Mark Eckel clearly and convincingly shows how all worldview beliefs affect teaching and learning. The book is unique in that it directly links insights about comprehensive Biblical integration with numerous activities and examples. Christian school administrators will find it a valuable tool for staff discussions and teacher professional development.

--Harro Van Brummelen, Dean, School of Education,
Trinity Western University

This is a book that every serious Christian must read. In a popular, easy to understand style, Mark Eckel explains the process of biblical integration, addresses the foundational issues of Christian worldview, and gives hundreds of examples showing God's world through the lens of God's Word. As Paul taught us in Romans 12:2, living Christianly begins with thinking Christianly.

--Joseph M. Stowell, President, Moody Bible Institute

The Whole Truth is an owner's manual for connecting Biblical truth with everyday learning. And an education without Truth steeping to its bones, is like junk food to the body—all fat and no muscle. Eckel's school and teacher proven strategies provide practical help for those who want to restore proper "Truth" nutrition for America's soul! I have seen him teach his doable approach to teachers, and I know it works!

--Ed Gamble, National Executive Director of the Southern Baptist
Association of Christian Schools

Mark Eckel has spent years of research discovering basic principles that provide biblical integration for any subject of study. His approach to biblical wholeness is a breakthrough in Christian education. Any teacher wanting to provide a quality Christian education will want to study this book and make use of its principles.

--James W. Braley, Former ACSI Director of Educational Services
Christian Education Consultant

Mark Eckel provides a practical guide in how to teach redemptively. This desperately needed book moves beyond just talking about Christian school philosophy to clearly modeling how thinking biblically is carried out in classroom activities. The "whole truth" is a practitioner's guide to effective biblical integration. It should be studied in every Christian teacher training institution, and by every teacher currently in the field.
--*Anne Rauser, ACSI Canadian Regional Director*

Christian educators have long struggled with knowing how to integrate faith in all aspects of their teaching. If we are to go beyond merely using the Bible as a rich source of examples and general moral principles, we must undergo a total transformation of our thought and practice. Mark Eckel has provided the practitioner with a tool that will help reshape our thinking about the place of faith in the teaching of all of God's truth. His insightful questions and well-constructed activities challenge us to submit every aspect of the teacher-learning process to the authority of the truths revealed in Scripture.
--*Marta Alvarado, Ph.D., Chair, Department of Educational Ministries Moody Bible Institute*

Mention the words "biblical integration" to most Christian teachers and the first question is usually, "How?" How do we infuse biblical truth into *every* aspect of learning, make it accessible to all ages of students, and assure that they own it, too? Biblical integration may be the hardest thing we ever do as Christians, but it's unquestionably the most crucial. Mark Eckel's approach, arising from his experience both as a classroom teacher and a teacher consultant, provides us with concrete, workable, even transformative, solutions to the biblical integration challenge.
--*Teresa Mattson, Cheri Smith, Noelle Martell, Colleen Averill, and Sue Howard, Teachers at Lenawee Christian School, Adrian, Michigan*

The most compelling reason for the existence of Christian schools is to advance a Christian worldview. However, a huge disconnect exists between the theory of biblical integration and the practice of it. This book addresses this disconnect head-on. In addition, Mark Eckel correctly points out that "before one can practice [biblical integration].... Christian doctrine must form the basis for thinking and thus for teaching." Thankfully Mark gives us both theory and practice.

--Nancy Zins, Headmaster, Ad Fontes Academy, Northern Virginia

Mark Twain had the weather in mind when he wrote "everyone talks about it, no one does a thing about it" but the same has been largely true concerning the integration of faith and learning. Mark Eckel has done something about it! A "must read" for the Christian teacher.

--Timothy C. Evearitt, Professor of Education, Covenant College

The Whole Truth

Classroom Strategies for Biblical Integration

Mark Eckel

Associate Professor of Educational Ministries
Moody Bible Institute

Forward by Charles Colson

XULON PRESS

Xulon Press
www.XulonPress.com

Xulon Press books are available in bookstores everywhere, and on the Web at www.XulonPress.com.

Table of Contents

Forward by Charles Colson

There was a time when the word "worldview" was unknown to most people. If they heard the word in conversation, many would have been uncertain of its meaning or its implications. In fact, there was a certain academic quality to it. But that is no longer the case.

Over the past few years, it has become commonplace for politicians, pundits, and television news anchors — as well as pastors and teachers — to speak of the approach influencing certain policies or actions as a "worldview." While there would be disagreement about the essential elements of such worldviews — obviously not everything labeled *worldview* these days would accord with a Christian perspective — nevertheless, the idea that our view of the nature of life and the purpose of existence entails a comprehensive "life and world view" has become an accepted feature of belief systems in the West today.

If there is any risk in this situation, it is the fact that the term *worldview* is in danger of being exploited by anyone and everyone with an ax to grind or an agenda to push, no matter how alien the belief system may be. Extreme environmentalists, for example, have a worldview. Middle-Eastern terrorists have a worldview, of sorts. And those who honor Judeo-Christian culture have another, and certainly very different, worldview. The stark contrast between each of these organizing systems illustrates the way that fundamental differences of thought and belief shape behavior, and it offers us a caution to be judicious and discriminating in the value system that we claim as our own.

The challenge for Christian parents and educators today is clear. First, we are to help our children recognize that we all have a worldview — it's part of our basic equipment. Second, then, is the process of forming and shaping the particular beliefs upon which young people's lives will be built. This means that teachers and parents, themselves, must have a comfortable grasp of the

iv

essentials of a Christian worldview, along with a systematic approach for introducing others to it. But despite the fact that many individuals and organizations have tried to do this, the teaching principles and the general pedagogy of most Christian worldview studies is still in a state of confusion, and in need of reliable criteria and standards. Which brings us to the materials at hand.

The approach presented in this volume, by Christian educator Mark Eckel, has been tested and proven in classrooms around the United States with great success. By presenting the essentials of the worldview curriculum in discreet, ordered, and clearly defined sections, Eckel has been able to make the application process not only logical but also enjoyable. He has designed the text materials, throughout, to be engaging and consistent, so that both teacher and pupil will be able to transform ideas into a meaningful lifestyle.

For many, this text may be their first encounter with the world of ideas, and the task of grappling with arguments and counter-arguments may seem, at first, daunting. But this is the real value of Eckel's approach, taking the intellectual concepts systematically and in order so that the lessons are clear and practical. No student who is introduced to this approach in an applied and orderly manner can fail to become a better thinker, and, in turn, a better defender of what they believe.

Ultimately, any course in Christian worldview thinking should make the student a seeker of truth. Jesus tells us in John 8:32 that once we recognize the truth and "know" it personally, that Truth will make us free. Surely this is the challenge we face as educators and parents today: To prepare the next generation of Christian students (and their teachers) to engage the world of ideas. And by virtue of a structured and disciplined approach to worldview thinking — like the one presented in these pages — to equip them with the intellectual tools to become accomplished defenders of the faith and advocates of the Truth that makes us free.

My friend Mark Eckel has given us a great weapon to use in training young minds to engage the culture with discernment and a well-grounded biblical view of life.

Charles W. Colson
Washington, DC

Preface

"The land can be redeemed."[1] George Washington Carver uttered these words as he contemplated how to revitalize overworked southern soil. In the same way, if Christian schools do nothing more than practice age-old pedagogies, reinventing tired pagan philosophies with a Christian sugar coating, then the land of Christian schooling will be barren. The restorative measure that reconditions the soil of young minds thus must be teaching students to think redemptively.

Biblical integration is the bedrock upon which the distinction between Christian and non-Christian schools must be built. Simply saying that one has a biblical philosophy of education is not enough. Christian mission statements cannot stand by themselves: the teachers must be practitioners of the mission statements. College education programs cannot just talk about Christian school philosophy; they must show how thinking biblically is done in practice. Ultimately, if daily classroom instruction in biblical integration is missing, then a school is Christian in name only.

Hence the audience for this book is twofold: (1) teacher programs in colleges that are training the next generation of Christian school teachers and (2) instructors already practicing their vocation in the Christian academy. The present volume seeks to wed the philosophy of biblical integration with the practice of biblical integration. Biblical integration is hard work. Therefore, many concrete examples will be used to facilitate understanding of the ideas.

The definition of biblical integration cannot be left up to the individual. Descriptions may vary, but definition may not.[2] Any work, including this one, is a product of someone's point of view. That said, it is paramount to note the limitations of the study:

- The hermeneutical process for every principle

vii

cannot be tracked because of space constraints. While a great deal of effort and time has been spent in order to be careful with the text of Scripture, the specificity of exegesis or even plotting the process followed for each statement made is not possible.[3]

- It also follows that this work is a general overview. It must be recognized that each idea presented is not necessarily investigated thoroughly. People whose specialties are addressed can take the discussion to deeper levels.

- Redeeming scholastic disciplines is difficult because Christians must work at thinking biblically. The purpose of this book is to help teachers reflect upon their scholastic disciplines as unified with Christian thought.

- Transitioning between knowledge and practice produces its own set of difficulties. Clarity is desired but may not always be achieved.

- And on a personal note, I know as soon as I send in the manuscript I will see a need to add to it the next day. This is a beginning. Further work is forthcoming and certainly welcome from others.

Many hands make light work. I am so grateful for my wonderful family—my wife Robin and my children, Tyler and Chelsea—who sacrifice time and patiently listen to ideas to make this help available to others. Douglas Osborn, whom I met in a Toronto meeting, lately has become a partner in the production of Biblical Integration Resources (www.biblicalintegration.com), adding his constructive criticisms to the manuscript. Dr. James Braley has been a support, mentor, and my *father of faith* since 1988: his comments work as salve to the soul. Long time colleagues and friends, Cheri Smith, Noelle Martell, Colleen Averill, Sue Howard, and Teresa Mattson, were instrumental in prompting many a study culminating in some of what is seen herein. I am grateful to ACSI for the opportunity to lead the *Biblical Integration Enablers* in the 2001-2002 school year that formed the core of this effort. Moody Bible Institute deserves recognition for allowing a great deal of travel that not only encourages people in Christian school ministry but makes connections for our students and their future placement. Katy Loyko, one of my Christian education students at MBI, did a thorough job of accumulating the evidence for each endnote. And my editor-son, Tyler, spent countless hours helping his father see the text through the eyes of others. Though many hands have affected the process, any mistakes are mine alone.

God has told His people that they were responsible to redeem the earth daily (Leviticus 25:24) but that there will come a day when He, the Redeemer, will reconcile all things to Himself (Job 19:25). George Washington Carver was right: the land can be and will be redeemed. May Christian schools and their teachers commit themselves to the practice of allowing biblical principles to redeem and permeate their instruction. All praise to The Father and The Son through The Spirit. Amen.

Mark Eckel
Associate Professor of Educational Ministries
Moody Bible Institute
September 2003

x

Introduction
The Whole Truth

In the general vicissitudes of life, people can feel disconnected. Language barriers don't help. A few funny English translations get the point across:

- A German campground announced: "It is strictly forbidden that people of different sex, for instance men and women, to live together in one tent unless they are married for the purpose".
- At a Paris hotel: "Please leave your values at the front desk."
- Entries in a Bucharest restaurant: "Cheesy dumplings in form of a finger," "Roasted duck let loose," "Beef beaten in country fashion," "Chicken roasted in spit," and "Chicken soup with droppings."
- An Italian inn: "Any day or night our chef will throw up his favorite pasta dish for you."
- A Rome laundry: "Ladies, leave your clothes here and spend the afternoon having a good time."

Confusion also happens in education. Art Marquardt, a former high school teacher, interviewed students in his community about religion, the purpose of life, racism, and suffering. He discovered that young people were at a tremendous disadvantage to provide answers to his questions. Why? Marquardt said, "...because they have no philosophical base from which to start...they are not tied into a religious institution that gives a foundation for forming values."[1] The communication of beliefs is virtually impossible without a common language, a common translation.

A Common Language

The need for understanding the common language of the world is emphasized in Ecclesiastes. Therein Solomon sets the stage for worldview study. An *under-the-sun* view of life, a view void of God, offers no meaning. Everything—education, work, pleasure, competition, money, and acquisitions—are unfulfilling in and of themselves. Ecclesiastes may seem to have a very negative tone because of its repetition of the word *meaningless*. But Solomon is actually just giving a counterpoint against which he can compare a life where God is involved and show that it *is* meaningful. All is meaningless, unless, God is involved from beginning to end. The wisest man ever to live marks his positive portrayal of life with a refrain—the chorus to his song—such as in Ecclesiastes 5:18-20:

> Then I realized that it is good and proper for a man to eat and drink, and to find satisfaction in his toilsome labor under the sun during the few days of life God has given him—for this is his lot. Moreover, when God gives any man wealth to accept his lot and be happy in his work—this is a gift of God. He seldom reflects on the days of his life, because God keeps him occupied with gladness of heart.

Ecclesiastes says there is *Someone* outside the world who is fully involved with and gives meaning to this world. Understanding His perspective helps us to properly understand—translate—all of life.

A Transcendent God

God's being *out of this world* is captured by the theological

2

term *transcendence*—God is separate from, outside of His creation. For God to be involved in the world and with humanity, He must clearly communicate with humans. And He has.

However, as with all communication, if comprehension is nonexistent, the meaning is lost. Even though God has communicated to humans by means of *both* His creation *and* His Scripture, the permeation of sin in all of life disrupts our reception of His transmission. Sin fragments the truth and leaves humans with only pieces when there should be a whole. For unbelievers, creation and conscience leave them without excuse. They are accountable for knowing that *Someone* is talking (Romans 1:20; 2:14-15). Though responsible, the pagan is mostly unresponsive. Some, however, do recognize that there is at least something beyond them, even if they are not sure what it is. Jeremy Sisto, who portrayed Jesus in a CBS miniseries, commented on the part in *TV Guide*:

> The more I talk about him [Jesus], the more I'm intimidated by the weight of it all. It's not like any other role. You don't go home, kick back, have a beer and say, "Hey, I feel great about today's work. I really captured the character. I *am* Jesus!"[2]

Others recognize that there is not only something beyond them but that this something is apart from and more important than who they are. Vaclav Havel, former president of the Czech Republic, expressed such a feeling in an address to Stanford University, "What unites all humanity is transcendence; someone above us, without which we would not be."[3]

This is why the worldview in Ecclesiastes is important: it shows us that God is transcendent from creation, that He has made creation, that He has given meaning to creation, and, therefore, that He alone can bring cohesion to the sin fragmented state that creation is in. It is Christians' responsibility to first understand the

3

wholeness of creation under God and then to share their God-given understanding with unbelievers in an understandable language.

A Worldview That Works

The beauty of the Christian worldview is that it actually works. It is based on philosophical thought that can be practiced and shown to be true. God is not merely transcendent, He is also *immanent*—He is close to and cares for His creation. As in Ecclesiastes, God glorifies Himself through humans made in His image and He is interested in people and their endeavors.

The world works because God cares about it. The world works because it is true. History, medicine, farming, architecture, and technology depend on universal design that informs earthly function.

A number of my former students use biblical principles in their vocations. For example, Kirk became a lawyer. We began emailing about the question, "How can a Christian defend someone he *knows* is guilty?" Our discussions went back to Pentateuch law showing the basis for judicial practices such as innocent until proven guilty, paying a debt to society, and the rights of the accused. Guy, a professional hunter, discussed with me the implications of protecting creation while providing food for inner city, poverty-stricken families from his wilderness hunts. John was interested in medical ethics and interacted with me about how to go about creating public policy that would protect the weak. Practicing the truth of God's immanence means applying transcendent biblical principles to the real world.

If Christian schools have any hope of preparing students to live in the real world, all disciplines must be founded on the grid of both transcendence and immanence. Academies that exist for the right reasons will not simply baptize pagan beliefs with a Bible verse and then teach like everyone else. Christian schools will wed heavenly authority with earthly operation to properly explain

4

reality. Biblical principles should permeate everything because everything is based on biblical principles. God's intention, to glorify Himself within creation, could begin to be recovered with these four over-arching principles:

1. Wisdom. God created the world with wisdom (Proverbs 8). Believers are called to apply Wisdom's truths in all realms of life.
2. Relationship. The Trinity existed in community and made the world to work in the same way (John 17:5, 24).
3. Mission. Task, goal, and work give people purpose and fulfillment as originally ordained by God (Genesis 2:15).
4. Design. Function allied with beauty was resident within The Garden for human pleasure and application   (Genesis 2:9).

The flood of sin's corruption within creation might be turned back with these four over-arching principles:

1. **Humility.** People must recognize that the world does not revolve around them; that God calls us to sacrifice (Leviticus 19:18).
2. **Justice.** Fair treatment of people and property is commanded for the benefit of all (Exodus 23:1-9).
3. **Change.** The transformation of individuals is only possible from an outside source (Ephesians 2:1-8).
4. **Hope.** Expectation for the future is the only reason to live and that which everyone longs for (Ephesians 2:14-15).

Herein is the start of classroom strategies for biblical integration in the Christian school classroom. We begin with The

Personal Eternal Creator—both transcendent and immanent—whose Word enables all powers and properties to operate properly in life (cf. Psalm 147:15-20). And we search for the translation of that Word to find the lost, fill the empty, and fulfill the incomplete in all subjects and studies, the duty of Christian schoolteachers (Colossians 2:2-3).

Chapter One
Everyone Believes Something

Want to start an argument? Talk about the next election! People get *really* upset about politics *really* fast! Views are often set in stone. Quarter is given to no one. Ask about the opposition and they are treated like the devil! A good case in point was the 2000 U.S. Presidential Recount. When the Supreme Court cast its 5-4 decision to allow Mr. Bush's 537 margin of victory stand in Florida:

> Critics argue[d] that politics influenced the decision. But that's true only in the semantic sense that for each of us, our politics are rooted in our view of the world....Most of us are evaluating [the judges] through the thick prisms of our own ideologies.[1]

How can politics be based on a view of the world? Just like sunglasses darken sunlight, so people approach the universe with established belief. Knowledge is based on the color of a person's lens. People see politics, history, love—*everything*—through their own lens. Joel Belz summarized the idea well:

> A person's "religion," in the end, is wherever he puts his ultimate trust. It might be the God of the Bible, or it might be a slightly edited god, or it might be Buddha, or it might be a federal program,

or it might be herbal remedies or sports or a tax-sheltered annuity or his children. Your religion is that which claims your ultimate confidence. It's the same with "faith-based" organizations. Every organization is faith-based for every organization has cast its ultimate confidence somewhere. The question isn't whether you have faith. The question is where you have put it.[2]

So how people look at life gives them personal certainty that their way is the right way.

People assume their beliefs to be true. This means that everyone is full of partiality and prejudice. What people communicate comes from the way they think. Commenting about journalistic fairness, Eric Burns suggested that media elites aren't the only biased people around. "We are all creatures of ideology, to one degree or another, and we all refer to our ideology as truth."[3] Everyone has preconceived notions. We tend to be sure of ourselves, sure of our world, and sure we're on the right side of truth. But what if we're wrong? Take the following quiz:

1. Who do we trust about cars, stocks, and medicine?
2. Why do we trust them with our transportation, money, and health?
3. When do we doubt what we have come to trust?

Consider the subsequent answers. Since no one can know everything there is to know, we have to place our confidence in someone who knows something about what we *don't* know. We trust "experts" with our valuable commodities because they are supposed to know more than us. But when information comes in that refutes or contradicts our prior knowledge, some "expert" is going to lose a client!

Faith Matters

Everyone trusts a certain view of the world just like they trust car manufacturers or stockbrokers or doctors. Everyone has a *worldview*. Every view of the world has three components: (1) everyone believes something (they have faith), (2) everyone begins somewhere (they make assumptions), and (3) everyone questions everything (they live a philosophy). And since another person's perspective on life will ultimately bump into our own, it would behoove us to understand the importance of worldview.

In the movie *Indiana Jones and the Last Crusade*, George Lucas wanted the viewer to understand that a person's belief is important. Toward the end of the film the hero, Indiana Jones, stands on one side of what looks to be an uncrossable chasm. Behind him his wounded father cries out, "You must believe, boy!" Seeing the human impossibility of obtaining a magic elixir in the cave on the far wall, Jones exclaims, "It's a leap of faith!" Harrison Ford's character grips his chest, holds a booted foot over oblivion, letting his weight fall forward. In utter amazement the adventurer stands on a natural bridge, unseen from the vantage point above. Indeed, the message of the movie *Indiana Jones and the Last Crusade* is simply, "ya' gotta have faith." But the obvious questions remains, "Faith in *what*? Faith in *whom*?" Faith has content. It's not just enough to believe, but there must be *something* to believe *in*! Some place confidence in themselves, the human race, the government, a leader, or a creed. Make no mistake, peoples' loyalty must lie somewhere, in someone.

Loyalty breeds assumption: our ideas are based on prior belief. The following classroom exchange makes the point.

Student: It's common knowledge that 'big business' is corrupt. Companies are only interested in the bottom line. The poor have only one hope; Government.

Instructor: But who creates wealth and jobs?

Student:	Business people.
Instructor:	Yes! And where does government get its money?
Student:	Taxes from its citizens.
Instructor:	Exactly! The only way the state can help the poor is to take my money and give it to someone else. Perhaps a better means of philanthropy would be through individuals, churches, and community conscious companies.

What assumption did the pupil assert? The government helps people best. And what assumption did the instructor support? The government should protect people who produce wealth for the benefit of others.

Assumptions Matter

Assumptions form the basis for our thoughts. Our preconceived ideas may stem from what we've been taught or where we grew up. Three caveats assess the limits of our presuppositions.

(1) *Assumptions could be true or false.* Just because something is believed doesn't automatically make it so. Santa Claus may seem real to children, but parents know the truth.

(2) *Assumptions are held consciously or unconsciously.* A person might be able to explain giving to charity. But if someone looked in the individual's checkbook to see where he spends his money it would show if he really followed through on what he believed about giving to the poor. Some folks can explain their belief. Most people simply act on their unconscious belief.

(3) *Assumptions are lived consistently or inconsistently.* A humanist might say people create their own standards of conduct.

If so, then why not lie, cheat, or steal if these are the standards? People might hold a belief that ethics should be left up to the individual but nobody can live that way. A lack of universal standards for the group leads to anarchy.[4] What happens when my standards conflict with yours or those of others'? From this viewpoint, individual or societal standards can only be judged by that person or group. That's why everyone is dependent upon another view of ethics originating outside themselves, a transcendent standard.

Youngsters construct their own presuppositions based on a limited understanding of reality. Consider the following false assumptions children may make:

- Adults never make mistakes.
- It's always someone else's fault.
- The television must be right or it wouldn't be on.
- It's in the book.
- If I have a reason to be disobedient, that's OK.[5]

Everyone begins with certain thoughts. The question is whether or not those thoughts are correct.

What a person presupposes as truth may need alteration. In the movie *Fallen*, Denzel Washington plays a cop who is confronted by an entity he cannot explain. Being chased by this otherworldly presence, the police officer turns to a theist, a believer in God, for help. Complaining that he is after concrete facts in a case, he is corrected by the believer in the supernatural when she says, "Aren't your 'facts' just a little resistant to normal interpretation?" Since the police officer judges the world *only* through his five senses, he doesn't see how there could be anything supernatural engaging his world. But the believer suggests that life must also be interpreted through the grid of that which we cannot be seen.

Belief leads to assumption, which leads to philosophy: a framework of questions that everyone asks about life. How people think about life will determine how they live it. Alston Chase demonstrated that Harvard's philosophy of education produced *The Unabomber*. Positivism believes that science will perfect humanity and that progress is good. In the 1950's Harvard:

> ...taught that reason was a liberating force and faith mere superstition; the advance of science would eventually produce a complete understanding of nature. But positivism also taught that all the accumulated non-scientific knowledge of the past, including the great religions and philosophies, had been at best merely an expression of "cultural mores" and at worst nonsense; life had no purpose and morality no justification.[6]

One's point of view, affects their philosophy of life, creating certain behaviors in their life. Since the unabomber didn't agree with others' positions on issues, and his outlook on the world gave no basis for right or wrong, killing people with mail-bombs caused no conflict with his conscience.

Philosophy Matters

Worldviews create a frame of reference for every decision and activity. Faith leads to assumptions, which produce a philosophy of life. Many distinct philosophies have the suffix *ism*. The suffix *ism* normally means a kind of belief (see chart #1). To achieve a practical sense of how *isms* work, think about why you agree or disagree with the following statements.

Ism #1
ABC News noted, "The collapse of the Soviet Union was a simple matter of economics."

Ism #2
"Private property abuses nature, attacks the poor."

Ism #3
"Dishonesty in tax reporting is OK; the government has enough of my money."

Ism #4
When the tragedy at Columbine occurred, Bill Clinton said the answer was more gun control. When school shootings erupted in Santee, California, George W. Bush suggested that the remedy to violence was, "A matter of the heart."

Chart #1: A Worldview Sampler
("ism" equals "belief")

Theism:	There is a god
Utilitarianism:	The greatest good for the greatest number
Animism:	Spirit beings reside in everything
Pantheism:	God is in nature
Dualism:	There are two co-eternal, co-equal gods
Atheism:	There is no god
Materialism:	Matter is all that matters
Humanism:	Humans are the beginning and end of all
Deism:	A god created the world, and then let it go
Naturalism:	There is nothing outside the material universe
Hedonism:	Pleasure without pain; freedom has no restraint
Relativism:	Individuals decide ethics
Pluralism:	All viewpoints are equal
Pragmatism:	If it works, do it
Perfectionism:	Humans can overcome faults and limitations

Ism #1: Naturalism and the Nightly News
Some might argue that events in history are not generally explained by single causes. Comments here about the Soviet Union's collapse certainly leave out any supernatural explanations. Based on her personal interviews with those behind The Iron Curtain Barbara Von Der Heydt claims **prayer** as an unacknowledged factor which motivated communism's demise in her book *Candles Behind the Wall.* Certainly the work of President Ronald Reagan and Pope John Paul II could also be included as agents used by God to prompt the internal collapse of a corrupt, totalitarian system of government.

Ism #2: Materialism and Private Property
Statements such as this, from an extreme environmentalist point of view, forget a salient truth: people take care of what they own or use. Who spends the most money to take care of natural resources? Hunters. Why? Because they have the most to gain and the most to lose from how animals and land are treated. To understand this truth, watch how Johnny treats something that has purchased with his own money versus how he treats property that mom or dad has given to him!

Ism #3: Pragmatism: Stealing is Acceptable Unless We're Hurt
"If it works, it must be true," stops *working* when it directly hurts us! The obvious answer, "Stealing is stealing," should be the Christian response. Pragmatism is cemented in our human natures. *Just do it* is fine when you're adjusting a golf swing. However, "If it works, it's OK" has awful consequences when applied to ethics.

Ism #4: Perfectionism and School Violence
Worldview even affects U. S. presidential policy. President Clinton was in favor of external controls to quell violence. President Bush believed internal restraints were the first line of defense to stop murder. The first sought answers through

14

perfectionism: outside human rules make people better. The second believed that a person's intrinsic motivations needed the first correction. Christians should begin with the premise, "The problem isn't *out there*, it's *in us*."

What do these worldview interactions teach? *Belief always affects behavior*. Belief affects thoughts, attitudes, and actions. Belief affects interpretation of the news, understanding of history, and political leanings. Belief affects how people are treated, where money is spent, and how teaching takes place in the classroom. The fact that I chose *these* examples shows a belief of my own. Ultimately, Christians must acknowledge that their worldview is the determining factor for everything.

Chapter Two
Everyone Believes Their Beliefs Are Important

Every year since its inception (1997-2002), I have spoken on worldview at the Young America's Foundation High School summer conference. At the conference we examined various systems of thought noting their similarities and differences. Each year, the participants—whether Buddhists, atheists, or Christians—have been confronted by the fact that their worldviews, whatever they were, began and ended with *doctrine*. Doctrine is a set of statements that organize one's beliefs about the world and life.

For as long as I taught high school Bible (or Christian Life and World Studies—or CLAWS—as I called it) people would say, "You must not be able to teach doctrine in an interdenominational Christian school." I would always smile and ask folks, "What is the name of our school?" "Well, it's _____ Christian School!" And my rejoinder was, "As soon as you say the word 'Christian' you are stating your belief, your doctrine."

Doctrine produces worldview. Worldview leads to action. People act their worldview. Thus, how people act is based on their doctrine. Heterosexuals and homosexuals have doctrine. Liberals and conservatives have doctrine. Buddhists and Muslims have doctrine. Government and Christian schools have doctrine. Everyone has doctrine[1].

I would encourage my students to go to the University of Michigan in Ann Arbor. "Stand out on the street corner," I would begin, "and ask people, 'Who is Jesus?'" Take a clipboard along to keep a survey of your findings. You'll be amazed at how varied the responses you receive will be." I still remember the looks on their faces, eyes as big as saucers upon their return. "Mr. Eckel! You wouldn't *believe* who people think Jesus is!" I sat in rapt attention as they would regale their discoveries to me. In some way or another they would conclude, "Knowing what and why you believe yourself is so important!"

Doctrine shapes everything, including education. Moses, Socrates, Plato, Aristotle, Augustine, Aquinas, Comenius, Luther, Calvin, Rousseau, Dewey, Skinner began with what they believed to explain how they would teach. Idealism, realism, humanism, behavioralism, or any famous school of education is founded upon what people believe about the world. While instructing the next generation in Christian schools teachers need to keep this truth on their lips: *everything is theological.* That means that, since God gives meaning to everything, everything has its purpose within God and should be treated as such.

Indoctrination is a pejorative term in our culture. Schools of education abhor the word. They say, "We are to allow students to set their own course; our job is to facilitate the experiences of our pupils." But everyone communicates their belief system in what and how they teach. The permissive model coordinating student experiences is no exception. No one should be fooled. E*veryone indoctrinates; and everyone thinks that his or her indoctrination is right.*

Everyone's doctrine is based on five basic questions in life that everyone asks: (1) What's real? (2) What's truth? (3) What's best? (4) What's human? (5) What's ahead? Christian schoolteachers must have Christian answers to these questions.

What's Real: The Study of Existence

Students were returning from video interviews at the local college. They were to have asked passersby questions concerning 'what is real?'. Each group in turn reported their results, brimming with excitement after interacting with those of other worldviews. One young woman in particular began her oral report this way, "The artist Escher draws beautiful buildings with staircases leading in every direction...and going nowhere. Today, for the first time, I saw 'Escher-people': groups who believe so many things which take them down so many roads...to nowhere." People airbrush reality by making the world mean whatever they want it to mean, whether it has a purpose or not.

An example of people questioning reality and trying to find meaning in it is *The Matrix*. As a modern action science fiction film, *The Matrix* epitomizes the issues of reality. The main character is a computer addict who discovers a world within the world of cyberspace. He soon finds that the world he thought to be true was merely a fantasy planted in everyone's mind by nefarious machines that don't want people to know what is the true reality. Throughout the movie the creators ask their audience, "Are you sure you know what is really real?"

Christian reality flows from the biblical doxology "for from Him, and through Him, and to Him are all things" (Romans 11:33-36). We are responsible to The Personal Eternal Creator who has begun, sustains, and will culminate, that which is "visible and invisible" (Colossians 1:16). He is not only the source of creation, of reality, but He also infuses it with meaning. Answers to the questions that all students—in school and of life—ask, "So what? Who cares? Why should I study this today?" are all wrapped up in The One Who gives reason to life.

Reality is defined by the incarnation; Jesus came in flesh. As Madeleine L'Engle has said, "The incarnation dignified matter forever." The fact that Jesus came to earth in physical form demonstrated to all that the physical world was worth saving. Christian educators ought to have their students study *what is* because of *Who is*.

What's Truth: The Study of Knowledge

What do these three anecdotal statements have in common? First, a student emailed his professor. The smiles could be seen in every word. "Do you remember when we discussed in class that an evolutionist can't be a good environmentalist? Well, I used that on my biology professor the other day. He didn't like it at all. But he didn't have anything to say either!" Second, "The best definition of an atheist might be a person who wants their child to grow up in a Christian environment." Finally, "Mathematicians need precision for proof, but humanist mathematicians point to their fallen selves as precision's origin."

The essential point of these statements is this: people want something for nothing. It's called *benefit without cost*. Unbelievers assume the truth of the Christian worldview. They assume that since it's here I'll use it without bothering about its origins. But concerns remain. Evolutionists must concede that saying, "the strong survive" is incompatible with "protect the weak," which is the environmentalists' main cause. Atheists do not have a basis for Christian ethics without the Christian God: they cannot have the fruit without the root. And anyone using rulers and calculators measure based on a standard of *rightness* set by The Creator.

There has to be a source of ultimate truth. The statement, "Truth is up to me," can be made, but as soon as it's uttered, it sounds empty. The television commercials can say, "The more you know, the more you'll grow." But knowledge without truth is meaningless. Amounts of knowledge can be measured through testing, yet the obvious question is, "Who says *that's* important?" Ultimately, knowledge belongs to God because God knows all (Isaiah 40:13-14, 28). The Almighty made humans to receive and interact with His own revelation so that people might know Him (Jeremiah 9:22-24).[2] At the same time that God is knowable He is also *beyond us* (Job 11:7-8). So everything that we know must be interpreted through the revelation that God Himself has given to people since what can be known about God must come from God (1 Corinthians 2:7-13). Hence to know anything, humans are dependant upon Scripture (Romans 16:25-26).

The Christ's lordship over knowledge is true whether people acknowledge Christ or not (Colossians 2:2-4). Any truth in the world, then, arises out of a Christian base. Ultimately unbelievers must incorporate the truth they have from a perspective with which they disagree but cannot live without. It is incumbent upon the Christian schoolteacher to draw the line in the sand. If God created knowledge in the first place, then one must teach that interpretation of knowledge originates from The Creator.

What's Best: The Study of Ethics

Parental complaints. Student misbehavior. Sixty-hour weeks. Extra duties. No immediate changes in students from classroom instruction. Why do teachers do it? To most instructors, education is not just *a job*. Teachers teach because they think what they have to offer is truth. And from where is this perspective gained? Everyone acts on what they believe. Belief affects behavior. For the Christian schoolteacher, there is a sense of right and wrong, of *oughtness*, which arises out of a changeless authority.

Many have succumbed to the prevailing belief that truth is individual, relative, and popular. And once truth has lost its mooring, ethics are not far behind. If *Someone* is transcendent, and He has spoken, then His eternal nature has surely set the standards by which we live. The following diagram illustrates that ETHICS (*What is right and wrong?*) and AUTHORITY (*Who says?*) are based on TRUTH (*What is verifiable?*). But without IMMUTABILITY (*Is there an unchanging standard?*) and TRANSCENDENCE (*What is the source of knowledge?*), there is no reason that we *should do anything!*[3] Only The Creator is

20

changeless (Numbers 23:19-20), separate from, and outside of His creation (Isaiah 40:21-26). (The acronym EAT IT may serve as a mnemonic device to remember this diagram).

Diagram #1

The Christian school has a basis for ethics, authority, and truth. All other institutions pull their certainty out of thin air, or once again, base it upon the Christian worldview without attribution. The basis for any decision of *right or wrong* whether they are judgments of history, science, literature, math, or behavior arises distinctly out of a Christian ethic. What is best is not always easy. What is easy is not always right. What is right is not always popular. What is popular is not always (ever)lasting. Christian

21

school educators stand *under* the authority of Scripture and *over* the falsehood of relativism without excuse.

What's Human: The Study of Our Nature

"Children want to learn. True or false." This statement was written on the blackboard. The classroom of teachers began excitedly wagging their heads up and down until a large circle was drawn around *false*. The gasp was audible. "How does what we believe about human beings affect our approach in the classroom?" the instructor asked. How does Christian teaching about the inherent corruption of human beings matter in education? To assume children want to learn is to subscribe to the romantic humanist idea that children are innocent—good at heart! They are not. None of us is (Ecclesiastes 7:29; Romans 3:10-12). Sometimes students ask, "Why do we have to take the test?" The one word answer is *sin*. People are not prone to work if they don't have to!

Now, on the other hand, the fact that we bear the stamp of our Creator suggests that we also have a proclivity toward knowledge (Job 28:12-28). Our interest in learning *can* be aroused! While we fight the truculent nature to do otherwise, we can move students through a disciplined regimen of instruction because "eternity has been placed in the hearts of men" (Ecclesiastes 3:11).

How instruction takes place bears on this issue. Understanding the nature of the learner alerts the teacher to difficulties, influences, learning modalities, and the like. Communication will never effectively reach everyone in a class all the time. However, concerted, prayerful effort to meet students where they are and take them where they need to be encourages reformation of their minds towards one with a biblical worldview.

Anne Frank said that people, deep down, are good at heart. Considering that she was suffering at the hands of an oppressive,

22

totalitarian regime when she said this, such a statement could be commended for sheer strength of belief. But, no matter how strong her belief, the inherent corruption of human beings cannot be ignored. People's hearts are crooked. Thus, the process of Christian education must always begin with the regeneration of the person (John 1:13; 3:3-8). We cannot save ourselves (Ephesians 2:4-5). But once we meet He *who cannot be known*, we can advance, mature, and grow in our Christian worldview "by the renewing of [our] mind" (Romans 12:2) with His *knowledge* (Colossians1:9-10). Our salvation is through Him in our whole person.

What's Ahead: The Study of the Future

We have been made for another time, another place, and another Person. Philosophers call this *teleology*. A plan, goal, and purpose exists for God's world. He is called "the first and the last, the beginning and the end" for a reason (Isaiah 44:6; Revelation 1:8). God authored world history in His plan book before creation (Psalm 139:16; Jeremiah 1:5). Understanding my life was established in the past for the present and looks forward to what's ahead is central to a Christian's view of life.

It is said that everyone who plants a tree believes in the future. Indeed. As a Christian, if it is acknowledged that matter is based on Spirit and history begins in eternity, focus should be on another world. Teaching about afterlife and judgment are key. If there is no consequence for activity now, there is no basis for ethics (Psalm 73:16-17). Hence, the imperative for Christian schoolteachers' instruction is that this life is not a dress rehearsal. As R. C. Sproul says, right now counts forever. What is done in this life is significant for the next.

A catechism statement concerning future things gives a good summation of the basis for teaching on things to come: I believe in passing on the truth of the Christian worldview to the next generation (Psalm 71:14-18; 78:1-8). I believe the only thing I can take to heaven with me is my children: whether they be *physical* or *spiritual* (Romans 8:14-17; 3 John 4). I believe because life is short but my responsibility is long (1 Corinthians 3:10-15; 2 Corinthians 5:1-10). I believe that eschatology teaches two things: holiness for the present and hope for the future (2 Peter 3:1-13). I believe that the apathy, cynicism, and fatalism of my unbelieving peers are evidence of a lack of resolution; we long for completion (Philippians 1:20-23). I believe I can live 40 days without food, 3 days without water, 5 minutes without oxygen, but not one second without hope (Job 19:25-27; Titus 1:2; 2:13).

So I say with *Toy Story*'s Buzz Lightyear, "to infinity, and beyond!" My God is, "from everlasting to everlasting" (Psalm 90:2). A culmination is planned: there will be "new heavens and a new earth" (Isaiah 65:17; 66:22; Revelation 21:1). And hope for eternal life is not a pipe dream but is based upon the intersection of eternity and history in Bethlehem (Matthew 2:1-6; Galatians 4:4). Only Christian educators can explain the connection between *these things* and *last things*.

What's the Answer?

My final session at Young America's Foundation was almost over. The students and I had just examined the results of worldview: common statements of belief that our culture offers often lack a unifying consistency. Two points were key: (1) The Contradiction of Worldviews and (2) The Consequences of Worldviews. I could read it in their eyes. The tension built. Finally someone asked the question: "Is there **any** worldview that holds it all together?" It was the questions for which I had hoped. "Let me tell you what I believe," my apologist's heart began. We added a third point to the list: (3) The Cohesiveness of Worldviews. I then went on to explain The Trinitarian Christian view of life as found in The Bible.

24

Chapter 3
Everyone Does Not
Believe The Same Thing

Muslims believe that individuals are born sinless and that evil is always an attack from the outside. Islamic assumptions concerning human corruption will affect interaction with and strategy toward other groups. Utilitarians who believe public policy should include the greatest good for the greatest number fashions decisions based on numerical superiority. Multiculturalists contend that all societies, stories, and life perspectives are equally valid. They believe that cultures set their own ethical standards that should not be criticized by other countries. These examples suggest teaching contrary to the basic tenets of the Christian worldview, namely, that humans are inherently corrupt, minorities should be protected, and universal ethical standards exist for all nations.

Christians must necessarily be aware of beliefs opposed to their own. Believers must constantly exercise discernment in this area or they may unthinkingly adopt the views of others and allow them to impact The Church. The faith, assumptions, and/or philosophies of others produce a pattern of life different from that of believers.

Activity #1 at the end of this chapter is designed to help you identify the basic worldview beliefs behind some common statements. You may use this activity to Christianly, critically evaluate why you agree or disagree with the statements and possibly identify what worldview they may represent. Consider the following examples. A commercial might advertise, "Thirst is everything. Obey your thirst." The assumption behind this ad might be described as self-indulgent. It says that physical needs are to exceed all others. Self-discipline seems to be set aside. Another example, "What's true for you may not be true for me." might be identified as relativistic. If no objective standards for truth exist, right and wrong are up for grabs, you could insist. Every statement, idea, or deed is established upon someone's view of the world.[1] You might find the ideas from Chart #2 helpful to complete this activity.

CHART #2: SOME COMMON WORLD VIEWS

Animism: spirit beings reside in everything
Atheism: there is no God
Deism: God created the world, then let it go on its own
Dualism: there are two co-eternal, co-equal "gods"
Hedonism: pleasure without pain; total freedom
Humanism: humans are the beginning and end of all
Materialism: matter is all that matters
Naturalism: there is nothing outside the material universe
Pantheism: "God" is in nature
Pluralism: the unity and equality of all viewpoints
Pragmatism: if it works, it must be right and good
Relativism: situations change; individuals decide ethics
Utilitarianism: the greatest good for the greatest number

Contradictions, Consequences, and Cohesiveness

Just as all worldviews are based on answers to five basic questions, so all worldviews must answer three basic challenges:

the fact that worldviews contradict; the fact that worldviews have consequences; and the fact that worldviews must maintain cohesiveness within the world. The following three sections enlarge on these three challenges and show their importance.

#1 The Contradiction of Worldviews

Two opposite beliefs cannot both be true at the same time. Logicians call this "the law of non-contradiction." For instance, either atheism (there is no god) or theism (god is there) is correct; both cannot be true at the same time. Hinduism teaches that all creation is a part of god. Christian theology contends that God is apart from His creation. Simultaneously Hindu and Christian teaching are diametrically opposed.

Truth cannot be subjective (relativistic) and objective (absolute) at the same time. Christian educators must be able and willing to dissect error from truth in order to show that the Christian worldview stands above the rest.

#2 The Consequences of Worldviews

Compare three filmmakers: Oliver Stone, Steven Spielberg, and Mel Gibson. Mr. Stone seems to approach his films from a humanistic point of view. He has reinvented or reinterpreted history in movies to his own preference such as *Platoon* (where Vietnam veterans are seen as drugged out baby killers) and *Nixon* (of which Chuck Colson, who was in Nixon's inner circle, has said that was not the Richard Nixon he knew).

Mr. Spielberg's Hebrew background suggests a high view of history. Hence, *Schindler's List, Amistad,* and *Saving Private Ryan* are examples of verity in history from a man whose heritage demands such ideals.

Mr. Gibson is instructed by his Catholicism. Themes of family, courage, freedom, sacrifice, and loyalty—all Christian themes—resonate through *Braveheart, The Patriot,* and *We Were Soldiers*. Ideas establish politics, science, journalism, literature,

27

filmmaking, and every concept taught in school. People always act on what they believe.

#3 The Cohesiveness of Worldviews

Out of all the religions and spiritualities in the world, only the Christian worldview has the answer for the question, "Is there any worldview which holds it all together?" Since the establishment of the Christian worldview in Genesis, God has told His people that there is a unity of all things through Him. Thomas Cahill in *The Gifts of the Jews* suggests that Old Testament laws tell us the Jews were "the first people to develop an integrated view of life and its obligations...they imagined that all of life, having come from the Author of life, was to be governed by a single outlook." Cahill then writes a commentary on the *oneness* of Deuteronomy 6:4:

> The great formula is not that there is one God but that "God is One." From this insight will flow not only the integrating and universalist propensities of Western philosophy but even the possibility of modern science. For life is not a series of discrete experiences, influenced by diverse forces. We do not live in a fragmented universe, controlled by fickle and warring gods...Because God is One, life is a moral continuum—and reality makes sense.[2]

Christians follow Hebrew truth contending that wholeness or integration in their worldview is premised upon the wholeness of God's person.

Comparing The Christian Worldview with Other Worldviews

The subtitle to the article raised concerns: "The quest by adolescents for answers to profound questions about the meaning of life can be supported by encouraging spirituality in

28

classrooms."[3] The Association for Supervision and Curriculum Development's flagship journal was dedicated to *the spiritual*. The commentary suggested that merely acknowledging anything spiritual in the classroom would morally benefit students. But if worldviews contradict and the contradiction creates opposition, it's not too hard to see that all *spirits* cannot be *created equal* (1 John 4:1-6). Comparisons between things spiritual should be made and evaluation should take place. A Christian is then able to determine whether a spiritual teaching is true or not. Merely saying that *spirituality* or *being spiritual* is the key to anything in life, including education, is misguided and shortsighted. Consider the following philosophies.

Monism

This view of life stresses sameness over difference, unity against diversity. Everything is god. Obviously, for the Christian, the Creator—creature distinction is lost. Humanities' role as a vice-regent of God to subdue and rule the earth (Genesis 1:28; Psalm 8:5-8) would be nonsensical. And the *all roads lead to God* argument would only be biblically accurate were we speaking of all roads leading to God's judgment!

Dualism

The *yin-yang* symbol is a pictorial identification of the equality between good and evil. The old Gnostic heresy that "the flesh is bad" is suggested by the separation of spirit and matter as light and dark shapes. *Star Wars* best exemplifies the good-evil dualism in popular culture. If dualism is true, there are people, places, and events outside of God's control, because good and evil have no bearing on one another except in co-equal, co-eternal conflict. Suddenly Satan is responsible for "bad things" and is equal in all ways to God. Final victory and defeat are never decided—there is only eternal conflict. Yet the Scriptures say that Jesus' coming *in flesh* thwarts the *spirit over matter* charge (John

29

1:14). Satan is used by The Almighty to fulfill His plan (cf. Job 1, 2), and that certainty of triumph is guaranteed (Colossians 2:15).

Fatalism

The opening scene of the movie *Reality Bites* has Winona Ryder's character forced into concluding, in a valedictorian speech at her college graduation, that she is unsure of any future answers or hope for world problems. The audience responds with an ovation. "Que sera, sera," whatever will be, will be, creates a pervasive sense of darkness in the world. The dismal belief that there's no real reason for trying because things are already, inexplicably set in an unalterable direction stands in stark contrast to the Personal Eternal Creator whose providence is caring and controlling (cf. Psalms 104, 107; Ecclesiastes 3:12-14; 5:18-20).

Determinism

In *Forest Gump*, Tom Hanks plays a simple man who has experienced extraordinary adventures. Standing by the graveside of his wife he recounts, "I don't know if we have a destiny, or if we're all floating along on the breeze...maybe it's both." Arbitrary reasons for life such as these are unsatisfying because humans need to have meaning for life. The world does not work chaotically. We can count on normal processes to satisfy a predictable pattern of living. Laws of biology and business, meteorology and manufacturing, astronomy and agriculture work in ways that can be anticipated. Far from a mechanistic accident, the Christian can say that God's provision gives the cosmos stability through His governing of natural law and His personal superintendence and intervention (cf. Genesis 8:22; Leviticus 26:4; Jeremiah 31:35-37).

Narcissism

"A man must serve something outside of himself...otherwise, what is he? A man without a master." An interchange between spies in *Ronin* suggests not only the theme of the movie but the need that everyone has for transcendence—an authority beyond himself. The Christian view of life is premised upon God's love for us and our reciprocal love for Him. This is demonstrated through others' centered service. Self-indulgence, individualism, and greed, all ideas of narcissism, are antithetical to everything Jesus taught His disciples (Mark 10:35-45).

High alert. That's where Christian *mental detectors* should be set as believers seek to think biblically in an unchristian atmosphere. Understanding enemy tactics is imperative. By being discerning about other worldviews, Christian teachers will be better equipped to teach and help their students live their lives with a Christian worldview. Awareness of how these other philosophies came into being would help us get back to the root of the problem.

From Where Do Worldviews Come?

"*How* did we ever get here?" is a common complaint of students trying to grasp the concepts of *isms*. How false worldviews came into being can be summarized in a word: sin. Human corruption distorted all truth given by God at the creation. Truths about single aspects of creation—humans, the earth, matter, pleasure, and activity—often becomes a philosophy in and of itself. In Genesis 1 and 2 pure Truth exists. But Genesis 3 introduces the problem of sin and Truth is shattered into many truths that sin also corrupts to form falsehood (see Diagram #2). Here are some examples of the creation of isms:

1. Instead of understanding humans as created beings, humanism teaches that we only answer to each other and ourselves.
2. Pantheism necessitates that God is a part of the world rather than its Creator and Controller.
3. Instead of material things being for human use and enjoyment, getting more stuff is the end-all and materialism results.

31

Diagram #2 The Origin of Falsehood in Worldviews

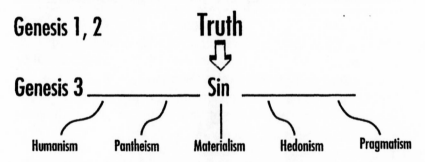

Genesis 1, 2   **Truth**
⇩
Genesis 3 _____ Sin _____

Humanism   Pantheism   Materialism   Hedonism   Pragmatism

There is some truth in every falsehood. That's why some worldviews sound good at first. But like veneer covering particleboard, there is a little truth and a lot of error. Christian truth provides the core or essence of truth for other viewpoints. When a *piece of truth* is appropriated by an *ism* it then becomes the whole truth, rejecting both the Christian base and the rest of Christian truth. Stated succinctly, unbelievers are dependent upon Christian truth. The basis for order, ethics, and purpose in any worldview all find their origin in Scriptural principles.

Diagram #3 The Origin of Truth in Worldviews

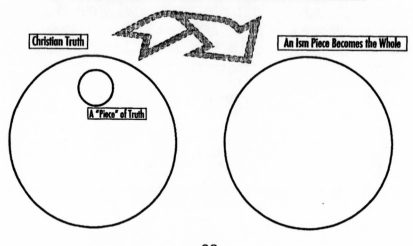

Christian Truth

An Ism Piece Becomes the Whole

A "Piece" of Truth

Because the Christian worldview stands outside and apart from other systems of thought, it can discriminate between truth and error (see diagram #4). There is no pluralism of worldviews: one is not just as good as another.[4] Jesus' statement marking Himself as "the way, the truth, and the life" (John 14:6) separates the Christian worldview from any other viewpoint. But people don't like that. Matthew 7:1 is often used as a bludgeon for tolerance. Jesus' comment, "Do not judge, or you too will be judged" is a statement against a judgmental attitude. Context tells us that judgment of what people teach is necessary. Jesus mandated in his distinctive message and words to watch out for errant worldviews (Matthew 7:15-27).

Diagram #4 The Distinctive Christian Worldview

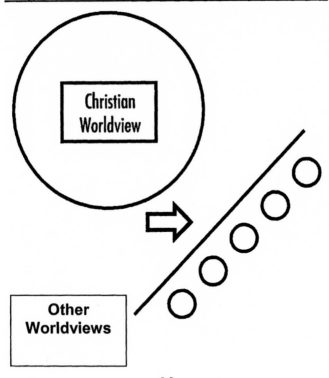

Biblical principles unify all truth because all truth is biblical. By reflecting the nature of The Trinity (three persons in one essence), only the Christian worldview can provide the answer to the question, "How does 'the one' and 'the many' fit together?" How do the fragmented pieces of truth fit to form the One Truth? Scholars in the Middle Ages introduced the *university* (*the one and the many*) as the place where people would come to study this very problem. Because of human sin, life became fragmented and disjointed. However, all pieces and parts, fragments and fissures, subjects and studies find their coherence, their *wholeness* in the Christian worldview.

Diagram #5 The Cohesive Christian Worldview

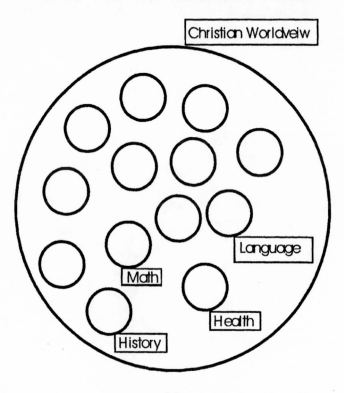

Pauline B. Johnson put it this way:

> Rene Dubos, bacteriologist, claims that "despite the immense diversity of creation, we all accept that there exists in nature a profound underlying unity." The unity of which the scientist is aware is also known to the artist who seeks the principles upon which relationships are established. This unity underlies the whole and is the framework for musical harmony, architecture, and all the other arts. It results from an orderly cosmos whose origin goes back to the God whose divine intelligence and creativity are manifested throughout the universe and through the creativity of man.[5]

Everyone does not believe the same thing. Popularity or personal opinion is a poor basis for authority. Attempts to deflect responsibility for behavior is an incomplete view of human nature. Suggesting that Jesus is acceptable as long as He is an equal among many spiritual leaders runs counter to the exclusivity of The Gospel. Christian, critical thinking is a matter of discernment. While loving all people as Christ loved us does not preclude "a pass" to instruction antithetic to Scripture. Engaging popular beliefs—identifying truth and error—is crucial for the Christian schoolteacher.

ACTIVITY #1: Whirled Views
Match the appropriate worldview with each statement.

Statement	Worldview
Life is short, drink it up.	
Be good. Be bad. Just be.	
Truth is evolving, revelation is ongoing.	
All views of life are equal.	
Society constructs reality.	
It's a dog-eat-dog world.	
Greed is good.	
Seeing is believing.	
Scientists tell us...Studies show...	
No one can save us but ourselves.	
If it works, do it. ("Just do it")	
Humans are perfectible: We get better and better.	
Education and knowledge are the fundamental catalysts for true change.	
Law merely reflects the tastes and preferences of the current society.	
If you can dream it, you can do it.	
Life is short: Play hard.	
The greatest good for the greatest number.	

ACTIVITY #2: It's Elementary My Dear Watson

This activity is designed to help you practice wholistic, Christian thinking. Christian teachers should always be ready with Christian teaching in a Christian classroom setting. Suggest a Christian doctrine that might answer each question.[6]

QUESTION	DOCTRINE
1. Why did this happen?	
2. Why am I like this?	
3. Where do we go when we die?	
4. Why is history important?	
5. Why does 'God' matter?	
6. How can I know if the author is right?	
7. How can I believe the news report?	
8. Why do people do bad things?	
9. Is it my fault?	
10. Why do people do good things?	
11. Am I different from my dog?	
12. What happens next?	

Chapter 4
Everyone's Belief Affects His or Her Educational Practice

I always turn to the back of the morning paper to read the comics first. The news of the day can wait until after the cartoonists explain the world in their strips. Students stop outside my office just to read my door and walls, plastered with funnies. Some are held by magnets to my refrigerator at home, others are taped around me in my study, re-created on overheads for presentations, additional strips are framed and under glass. These modern drawings capture philosophy through art.

The World According to Comics

Comics like *The Wizard of Id, Calvin and Hobbes,* and *Frank and Ernest* do a good job of explaining human nature. Of all the comics I've saved over the years those that communicate best are depictions of characters that correctly mirror what people are like. In *Non Sequitur*, Wiley Miller produced a comic titled "The Essence of Human Nature." A man and a woman are standing by a sign that says, "Absolutely NO Machete Juggling." The man comments, "Suddenly I have an urge to juggle machetes..." Chris Browne's *Hagar the Horrible* makes the case another way. Hagar's wife sees her husband leaving the house loaded down with weapons. "Where are you going?" she asks. "I'm meeting with Attila the Hun to discuss the possibility of a peace treaty." Frowning, her second question is, "Why do you need all those weapons?" Hagar matter-of-factly explains, "It might not be possible." In discussions with his boy, Hagar insists, "Never turn your back on an enemy, my son!" Reasoning with his father the child responds, "You should be more trusting Dad! He's not an enemy—he's a 'human being,' just like you." Making his point Hagar rejoins, "THAT'S why you should never turn your back on him!"

It sounds like these cartoonists have been reading Scripture! What better portrayal of biblical truth could there be? *Non Sequitur* is a mirror image of Genesis 3: we want what we have been forbidden to have. *Hagar the Horrible* goes on to add that issues of trust and peace are restricted not by human misunderstanding or weaponry but **by our nature.** The obvious question left to ask is "What makes us what we are?"

The Root of the Problem

Jesus' comment to the Pharisees in Mark 7:20-23 identifies the root problem of human relationships. "What comes out of a man is what makes him unclean." In theology this is called *inherent corruptibility.*[1] Everything about us is distorted, deformed, and disfigured. Thoughts, attitudes, and actions are in the all-inclusive category of our bent, twisted, and warped selves. Even the things we can hide from each other—our purposes, motivations, suggestions, or desires—are twisted and tainted by our sinfulness.[2]

Pointing fingers in all directions I make the point to my students. "The problem of sin is not out there," I say. I tap my temple and whisper, "it's in here." I am happy to find not only comics but also articles, films and books that agree with this point of view. In reviewing the film *Lolita*, based on Vladimir Nabokov's classic tale about a man's obsession over a twelve-year-old girl, AP writer Frazier Moore said,

Indeed, the power is in what's left unshown, what the film sets unreeling inside of you. There, if anywhere, is where the ugliness resides. [Is] *Lolita* shocking? Nothing it displays will infect you with thoughts and urges you don't already have. Those, not the film, are liable to be shocking.[3]

Charles Colson also gave us a glimpse at our internal sordidness when he told the story of Yehiel Dinur,

A Nazi holocaust survivor, [who] was a witness during the trial of Adolf Eichmann. Dinur entered the courtroom and stared at the man behind the bulletproof glass—the man who had presided over the slaughter of millions. The court was hushed as a victim confronted a butcher. Then suddenly Dinur began to sob, and collapsed to the floor...but not out of anger or bitterness. As he explained later in an interview, what struck him at that instant was a terrifying realization. "I was afraid about myself," Dinur said. "I saw that I am capable to do this...exactly like he." The reporter interviewing Dinur understood precisely. "How was it possible for a man to act as Eichmann acted? Was he a monster? A madman? Or was he perhaps something even more terrifying...was he normal?" Yehiel Dinur, in a moment of chilling clarity, saw the skull beneath the skin. "Eichmann," he concluded, "is in all of us."[4]

Honest individuals acknowledge the darkness of their own person.

Excuses for Human Nature

Belief about human nature is the common denominator that differentiates liberals and conservatives. Liberals tend toward a human perfectibility point of view. Those on the left believe that money and government will help solve problems and make people good. Conservatives lean in the direction of human corruption. We are inclined to practice wrongdoing because we are given to rebelling against authority. Therefore, those on the right prefer an internal regulator from an outside source be the acknowledged standard. While Christians acknowledge the dignity of people made in God's image the need for reformation must begin from the inside out.

Belief in perfectibility is what instructs some cultural viewpoints. Three reasons are normally given for why we act the way we do: (1) biology—"I was born this way"; (2) environment—"I was brought up this way"; or (3) psychology—"I just behave this way". These excuses for why people murder, hate, covet, or steal deflect responsibility away from us. Suggesting that accountability lies within ourselves cuts against the grain of human perfectibility. Choice, decision, or *an act of the will* might indicate our own culpability—and we couldn't have *that*!

Caught drunk by the king in *The Wizard of Id*, the court jester intones, "Actually, sire…I'm suffering from a chemical imbalance." Genetic preconditions are often hailed as proof of a person's conduct. Though by no means accepted by all in the scientific community,[5] news reports often link biology to bad behavior. Reporters convey belief with statements such as, "Altruism, Not Aggression, is True in the Wild." Or when referring to homosexuality, "sexual orientation" is preferred to the phrase "lifestyle orientation" because the former suggests, "I can't help it, this is the way I am, I was born this way." Sloughing responsibility off onto biology leaves humans irresponsible for their actions.

Calvin, complaining that Santa is bias toward good kids at Christmas, contends to Hobbes that "mitigating circumstances" should be considered. Reminded that he had placed an incontinent toad in his mom's sweater drawer, Calvin defensively asserts, "If I was being raised in a better environment, I wouldn't do things like that." Next to biology, background is the answer for many who look for behavioral rationale. " 'Harsh Upbringing Shaped my Client,' Claims Defense Attorney" contends the newspaper headline. The idea behind this statement is that culture is responsible for creating the minds of people who live within its society. This can lead only to excising responsibility from individuals. In courts of law, for instance, the contention that a cruel upbringing shapes criminals is an important testimonial and can lead to the exoneration of a guilty offender.

While the "nature—nurture" (biology versus environment) debate continues, psychology has been added to the list of reasons for why we act like we do. Frank contends to a lawyer in a *Frank and Ernest* cartoon, "Take responsibility? Is that legal?" This comic pokes fun at the belief that it's just not psychologically healthy to feel bad for what you've done. Some would even like to explain one of the darkest days of American history, September 11th, 2001, this way:

> It might be more comforting to think that Atta was stark raving mad, but true madmen, who are usually dysfunctional, don't work with Atta's calm purpose. No one wants to think that even a seminormal human being—indeed, nearly a score of them— could do what the terrorists did on September 11. In a world of moral relativism, we prefer psychological explanations; no one wishes to stare directly into the face of evil.[6]

But even talk show host audiences draw the line somewhere. Maury Povich suggested that the self-exonerating theories for criminal acts based on psychology went over the line in the case of the Menendez brothers. In the process of killing his parents, while his mother begged for her life, Lyle Menendez calmly left to reload his shotgun reentering the room to inflict the fatal wound. "That,"

42

said Povich, "was the turning point for most viewers of this program. They knew this defied reason."[7]

Concerning the Lemak murder case in Chicago—where a woman drowned her own children—Elise Wachspress said in an editorial column:

> Lemaks' case has proven that evil is not necessarily stupid, poor, black, or ugly. It's not relegated to bearded ideologues in Asia or Central America, to drug dealers or gangbangers. It can flourish in each of us, and we each have the responsibility to look to our own behavior.[8]

While Christians should maintain that a person's internal makeup or external surroundings might *accentuate* their behavior, the root cause is forgotten. Scripture places the blame squarely on us. "There is no one who does good, not even one" (Ecclesiastes 7:20; Romans 3:12). A biblical worldview tears down the façade of excuses for our behavior. For Christians, answers to the questions like, "Why do we do bad things?" can only be explained Christianly. We must be careful so that our view of life is shaped not by our culture, but by our creed.

How many of the following statements are heard in the classroom or home:

1. "It's the way he was born."
2. "It runs in the family."
3. "Everyone does it."
4. "He can't help himself."
5. "He's on medication."[9]
6. "Rules stifle my son."

Guess where they come from? Every single one of these ideas has their origin in the environmental, biological, or psychological justifications explored in the last section.

How Do Worldviews Affect Teaching Methods?

Understanding behavior "worldviewishly" in the classroom is one thing. Teaching methods (*teachers'* behavior), how we have been taught to teach and what we teach, is another. Systems of faith, assumptions, and philosophies affect schools of education. There is no neutrality in any lecture hall. Educators subscribe to certain points of view that color their approach to teaching and to their students. Christian schools claiming a *Christ-centered curriculum* in their mission statements and hiring state certified teachers over those trained in biblical integration may have fallen prey to the allure of theoretical aptitude over and against abilities to discern disciplines Christianly. While there is nothing wrong with doctorates or credentialing, acclaim consigned largely to *them* places intellectualism before Scripture. Maintaining a Christ-centered curriculum and Christian interpretation of life is critical to making a distinctively *Christian* school.

Christian educators believe in sanctification. Learning is a process. To wit: first a child learns two plus two equals four, then she learns quadratic equations, next geometric proof, finally being able to lay tile in her basement bathroom. Understanding that knowledge built a little at a time arises out of the Christian understanding of progressive sanctification is important: change and maturation in life take place one step at a time (Romans 6:19; 2 Corinthians 3:18). This is just one example of an over-arching principle that demonstrates the difference between a Christian and a non-Christian approach to education.

A friend in government schools once told me that after nine years of teaching science he would be able to teach the same curriculum the next year—for the first time in his tenure! Why do schools constantly alter their textbooks? Because pragmatism—John Dewey's major contribution to American education—imposes change until something is found to *work*. Immediate supplants long-term. Truth becomes relative. Diversity trumps unity. Patience acquiesces to urgency. Usefulness outranks personhood. The end justifies the means. Infected by pragmatism we refer to our parents as *consumers* and our teachers as *human resources*. Communicating ideas such as these substitutes a dollar sign for the dignity of people saying, "we will use you till you're gone."

Missouri's motto of "The Show Me State" makes a good case for not believing everything one is told![10] But positivism has hijacked the necessity of physical evidence making technology the Supreme Being. Every reliable scientist knows verification is essential to proof, yet studies in the natural realm alone do not corroborate everything. Denial of supernatural intervention ignores the work of The Spirit. Lack of concern for the immaterial coarsens attitudes toward the immaterial nature of a child. Attention to only what can be identified with five senses begs the question of mystery and tension in finite life. The Christian educator is not limited to a *physical* or *spiritual* world. Informed and motivated by The One who lives within us (1 Corinthians 2:14,15), we help our students understand the unity of all God's world seeing life from his perspective.

Since everything is reflected in belief, teaching methods are not neutral. While none of the methods noted below are wrong to use, they either arise out of a specific thought pattern that, when taken alone, leads to corruption of truth or promotes a fragmented view of God's world.

Note how two methods of teaching—lecturing and discussion—are based on two separate philosophies of education. If the first person learns best by lecture, his proclivity in teaching will be toward lecturing. An objectivist could appreciate direct instruction since facts and authority are paramount. But, for an interpersonal learner, discussion might be the favored mode of teaching. A constructivist would enjoy discussion since their tenet is "students discover and experience their own truth." But lecturing alone could cause students to rely solely on what they're told and not develop the ability to learn or think for himself or herself. And with discussion, the neglect of meaning, absolutes, or authority could leave the student with the idea that personal opinion is of greater value than what any authority might say. A Christian philosophy, however, can rightly give reason for and combine the two. Since God is transcendent, He has authority over us. And because He made us in His image with the ability to think and reason, we have a responsibility to analyze what we've been told.

Laboratory experiments are essential to discovery and corroboration of data. However, intellectualism, scientism, and rationalism spawned the idea that humans could know everything by following the mantra of *the scientific method*. Results of this perspective in academia include statements about "academic excellence", while contributing to blind spots concerning the immaterial (e.g., "emotional" or "spiritual") needs of children. The promotion of inflexible classroom procedures and evaluations might be a result. Christian educators have the most to gain from technical research as they examine God's world while at the same time celebrating the sundry giftedness of our protégés (1 Corinthians 12:14-26).

Rote memorization is crucial for cementing key concepts such as times tables or foreign language declensions. But when only that which is factual, observable, and verifiable through the five human senses contains viable knowledge, positivism is the likely progenitor. Facts and memory are of first importance. Yet, personal, internal connections to knowledge must not be sacrificed. Opportunity for reflection through journaling, for instance, could augment specific information for students mirroring the Christian view that pondering over what we see around us produces praise and even godly fear (e.g., Psalm 64:9; 65:5-13; 66:1-7; 67:1-7).

The Great Books adorn many home bookshelves. Mortimer Adler's contribution of reminding moderns of ancient classic works was remarkable. But reducing essential ideas, models, or theories to one period of history or one group of writers is called perennialism. The Great Books approach, identifying certain volumes as more important than others, may sideline important truth of other times, places, and people. Obviously, Christians would expand the set to include the writing of believers such as Moses or Paul. While texts that have moved us toward more truth should be celebrated, we must be reminded that biblical revelation must rule human reason at all times.

Teaching methods are not neutral. Every means of training has been tainted by sin through one worldview or another. Christian school teachers should vary methodology not only because all students are different but more so because by only teaching one way, we may be subtly directing our students toward a deceptive perspective of the culture. Redeeming approaches to teaching is yet another responsibility of the Christian schoolteacher.

Chapter Five
Everyone Integrates
What They Believe

Everyone superimposes their belief system over whatever they see, hear, or read. It comes naturally. And it should. My daughter Chelsea wrote a paper on women's rights. She highlighted a truth often left out of the discussion—God's justice should be granted to all people. My son Tyler's position paper favoring free market economics was premised upon the divine character mirrored in human creativity, individuality, freedom, and will within the bounds of God's law.

Yet children in classrooms do not think Christianly just because they happen to be in a Christian school. Christian thinking does not come out of thin air. Any teaching about worldview that should impact the instructor must be passed along to their pupils. How young people are taught to interact biblically with their world is paramount. The first question to answer is, "What makes Christian school education distinct?"

Invasion, Investment, Inversion and Integration

There's been an invasion. Jesus came to the world to reclaim it. He came to the world to reclaim us. We are "new creatures in Christ" (2 Corinthians 5:17). The change that takes place in the life of a believer begins in the mind.[1] The Christian mode of thought is actually to be a counter-cultural movement.

Jesus was not interested in political correctness; he was interested in reclaiming everything for the truth, whether people liked it or not. For the Christian, everything is reclaimed by Christ's invasion. Money becomes a resource for eternal ventures rather than simply a commodity to be accrued for individual gain (compare Luke 16:9 and 1 Timothy 6:17-19). Athletics' primary focus becomes community discipleship, countering a culture's obsession with winning at any cost. As Jesus said, "What is highly valued among men is not highly valued with God" (Luke 16:15). Jesus has invaded this world.

Infiltration of Jesus' grace in one's life is His investment in us. Since He has invested in us, five major changes must occur.

1. We have a new conformity (Romans 8:29). Conventions and traditions are altered. Our focus is on Jesus' life, not our own.
2. We have a new mindset (Romans 8:5-8). Our outlook, attitude, approach to and style of life shifts. A "here and now" frame of mind becomes a "there and then" standpoint.
3. We have a new thought process (Philippians 3:10). Deliberation patterns abruptly reverse themselves. We care about Christ and His Kingdom, not our own power and glory.
4. I have a new attitude (Philippians 2:5). Posture and position change. Viewpoints reflect The Creator's perception over against private opinions.
5. We have a new distinctiveness (Colossians 1:28-2:10). We are not just set apart *from* something, but *to* something. We declare our allegiance not so much by what we're *against* but what we're *for*.

Invasion causes investment leading to an inversion. *Rightside-up* thinking is a good way to put it. Jesus' coming gave us a new system by which we may learn about and through which

49

we may live life (2 Corinthians 5:16). Jesus said, "I've come to change everything, turn everything right-side up" (*The Message*, Luke 12:50). Our Lord says things that capsize our thinking. Consider the following statement, "God helps those who help themselves". The world says this famous statement is true. But when we look into what Scripture says that phrase is totally turned around: "God helps those who **cannot** help themselves" (cf. Romans 5:1-8). By investing our energies in discovering the truth, we find that much of this world sorely needs to be turned right side up. Activity #3 at the end of this chapter offers an opportunity to practice *rightside-up* thinking.

But "turning the world upside down" (Acts 17:6, KJV) does not take place because someone has adopted New Year's resolutions. This inversion process leads to integration: a wholeness that informs the entirety of life, that affects the whole of teaching. Eric Liddell, trying to convince his sister of his purpose driven life in the movie *Chariots of Fire*, declares, "God made me for China. But He also made me *fast*! And when I run, I feel His pleasure." Liddell's life—his missionary endeavors and his 1924 Olympic competition—was given to His Lord. What matters is not a change in placement or profession but in our total person. The whole new way of thinking should have personal, vocational, and institutional effects. A poster hung in my classroom for years. It read, "It's not just about information, it's about *transformation*."

Intentional, Influential, and Transformational

The invasion, investments, inversion, and integration process raises three questions for Christian teachers: (1) Are we intentional? Do we plan to teach Christianly? (2) Are we influential? Do we bring others along with us in this educational venture? (3) Are we transformational? Do we think that what we do will change the world according to God's will?

Charles Habib Malik pronounced,

We founded our faith on Christian truth, Christian principles and then from that foundation we are free to explore, look, examine. We are free to study other things because we tie them and relate them back to the truth of God's Word. But once we cut out that foundation we have people in a moral drift, floating off in all directions, examining and exploring and not knowing how to get back to the reality of the God of creation. The foundation has been taken away.[2]

The first questions teachers should be asking ought to frame this Christian vantage point. The first concern of Christian schoolteachers should be to develop their own biblical philosophy of life. It is then their responsibility to deliver to their students a Christian understanding of the world. Reflecting on the questions in Activity #4 at the end of this chapter will help you evaluate your Christian understanding of the world.

There is a danger. Schools that trade their mandate of teaching Christianly to mollify affluent families, curtsey to government regulators, or bring in money sacrifice philosophy for cultural pressure. At times, Christian schools resemble nothing more than private schools. Some schools hire unbelieving college professors to teach Advance Placement courses. Others carry pro-choice faculty. Still others take whatever teachers they can find—sometimes adding skeptics to their staff.

Integration of any kind can never rise from theological ignorance. This has long been a major problem in Christian elementary and secondary schools as well as in Christian colleges. While requiring adequate credentials in a particular age-level or content specialization, we require only the most rudimentary biblical instruction. Schools often hire faculty with little or no formal training in biblical and theological studies, expecting that strong church affiliation and personal devotions will fulfill that side of the requirement. Such teachers can no more construct an evangelical world and life view than a practicing pastor can integrate Scripture and astronomy from watching several episodes of "Nova." The problem is exacerbated because the administrators who do the hiring and requiring do not themselves know the Scriptures intimately and, therefore, find that quality a less-than-demanding issue among their subalterns.[3]

Knowing what and why one believes is critical. Interpretation based on that knowledge must become second nature. Where that interpretation comes from must be understood.

Pragmatic scholasticism also invades the thinking of some. Christian schools that exist so that Johnny can get good grades, to go to a good college, to get a good degree, to get a good job, to make good money, to have a good life. A Christian label is not a Christian education. Academic standards are not a replacement for biblical integration. Where graduates attend university is not the focal point of why Christian schools exist. Degrees, test scores, professional placement, or the amount of take-home pay does not indicate success for academies built on a Scriptural foundation.

The Christian school is either Christian or it is not. The essential should not be sacrificed on the altar of the immediate. Since philosophy forms the basis for practice, biblical integration must rest on learned immutable truths. Charles Colson stated:

Christian [schools] have been a casualty of the radical individualism of our day, of the emotion that people have that Christianity is a private transaction between the individual and God; we really have no concern for a biblically informed world-view. We

52

come to Jesus, we're saved, and we live happily ever after...in a protected environment. Christian education has made itself out to be an education provided in the liberal arts or the sciences in a Christian environment where you have chapel and Bible studies and a code that kids are supposed to live by. This is done so that they can live in some kind of protected Christian enclave while they get the same kind of education they would have gotten at [another school]. Christian education has failed to make a convincing case that it is different from secular education, that we see all of education influenced by our understanding of revelation and truth from a Christian perspective, where every discipline is undergirded by a basically distinctive or Christian view of reality. If you're simply offering a Christian adaptation of what you're given in secular schools then I would probably be urging my grandchildren to go to secular [schools] which are better known and would give them a better shot at [further education].[4]

Some astute administrators have concluded, however, that their teachers do not know Bible doctrine, much less their Bible. When I teach about biblical integration the audience often receives it in shocked silence. It's not simply because what they've heard is overwhelming, it's because many are in over their heads. It cannot be stressed enough: before one can practice, much less understand biblical integration, Christian doctrine must form the basis for thinking and teaching. Taking additional coursework in Bible will help *if* the teaching is relational to God's world and relevant to both this life and the next. Courses heavy in Bible content are no substitute for those whose goal is to interpret life Christianly.

Training Christian teachers to think Christianly about their subjects is a lifelong process. Those who do the hiring in the Christian academy must be requiring believing educators to see integrative thinking as part and parcel of personal sanctification. Hence the person of the Christian schoolteacher is paramount. Teachers in the Christian school classroom should have a biblical worldview that is then replicated in all their teaching. Head hunting is commendable. Choosing teachers who already think Christianly, who will prepare lesson plans with the eternal, transcendent focus in mind is crucial. Teacher's committed to biblical integration are an administrator's dream.

Either biblical integration is the central focus of Christian schools —all other discussions radiating out from it—or the proper view is lost. One time when my phone rang, a principal at the other end of the line asked, "I have an hour to fill. Would you come and speak on biblical integration?" Another school leader who had invited me to present biblical integration to his faculty introduced my seminars by reminding his staff that understanding the world through The Word was a one-year initiative…along with diversity training and learning disabilities. But biblical integration should not be an hour-filler or even a year-filler: it must be the end-all of the Christian school.

If you plan for nothing, you'll hit it every time. While moments of inspiration do occur, biblical integration should be planned. It doesn't just happen. The following diagram shows how a plan for integration should look.

Diagram # 6: Integration Planning

**Lesson Plans
Curriculum
Admissions Policy
Christian Thinking Teachers
Biblical Philosophy of Classes
Mission Statement**

As the diagram suggests, integration moves from the ground up, starting with the basic idea (Mission Statement) and moving to the more complicated matter of day-to-day practice (Lesson Plans). Curriculum review as well as weekly lesson plans given to administrators must intentionally reflect biblical integration. Weekly faculty meetings should include a brainstorming session, ideas from master teachers, or administrative templates for biblical integration. Departments and grade levels must construct their own biblical rational for teaching their subjects Christianly.[5] Scope and sequence then begins to reflect a God-centered flow of thought. In order for this to be accomplished, Christian schoolteachers must be growing in their own understanding of Christian belief. Books, periodicals, tapes, visiting lecturers, refresher courses, and round-table discussions that shape a believer's worldview should infect the thinking of each educator. They must take it in before they can give it out.

Formatting school practice assumes that Christian teachers are committed to teaching Christianly, and that Christian administrators are committed to hiring them. The plain fact is that the same weakness afflicts most Protestant attempts at education:

...neglect of full reliance upon Scripture. And let it be noted, this is true even of the theologically conservative groups; in doctrine they are thoroughly Biblical, but they have failed to see that the great truths of Scripture embrace even the so-called secular fields of knowledge. Despite their adherence to fundamental gospel truth, they have either not seen the unity of all truth in God or, recognizing this unity, have done little to make it a living reality throughout the whole of education. Thus much of evangelical educational thought has yet to move beyond a kind of scholastic schizophrenia in which a highly orthodox theology

55

coexists uneasily with a teaching of non-religious subjects that differs little from that in secular institutions.[6]

It is difficult yet imperative to allow the sanctification process to change teacher's thinking and teaching. Even *The Chicago Tribune* noted obvious differences when a Christian school has the proper biblical approach.

"Families that select a school because of faith-based values do so because those values permeate the whole curriculum," says Gary Arnold, administrator of Harvest Christian School in Crystal Lake, Illinois. Barb Levant, a Catholic...sends her daughters to St. Ignatius and stated her agreement with Arnold's point this way: "Even a math problem at St. Ignatius has a deeper meaning in it...It's not just math and science. It's the 'why' behind things they teach that I like."[7]

Biblical integration is not one more thing: it's the main thing. Apart from a continual commitment to distinctive Christian teaching, Christian schools will become Christian in name only. Activity #5 is designed to engage the individual instructor or whole school staff in reflection over their dedication to biblical integration.

My administrative "hero" is Nancy Zins because she has pored over her teachers' lesson plans for years to help them with biblical integration. To shepherd people in any learning process one must make the commitment of time and resources to communicate the essentials of biblical learning. Encouraging teachers to practice Christian thinking must be incorporated in accreditation, peer review, curricular oversight, mentoring, and even contact in the hall between classes.

We have directors of athletics, admissions, and development, why not a director of biblical integration? Jessica Roberts served as the "Biblical Integration Director" in Niwot, Colorado. The staff at Rocky Mountain Christian Academy is so enthused about this teaching in biblical integration that their collective comment is "Why haven't we done this before?"

Everyone must be aware that a Christian school is committed to being Christian through and through. Board, parents, students, faculty, and staff, should be constantly reminded of the school's philosophy. Mimicking the real estate motto that emphasizes the importance of location, Christian school stationary, websites, memos, answering machines, calendars, and weekly letters home should "Communication, communication, communication!" Admissions policies should ask questions giving guidance that obviously communicates the vision of where the school is going. Parents should be required to read, watch, or be instructed in the philosophical foundations of Christian education on a yearly basis. As with educating people to remember, the cohesion of the school's philosophy is dependent on repetition. Activity #6 is a practical way of revisiting and reenergizing the purpose of a school's existence.

ACTIVITY #3: Comparing Viewpoints[8]

Jesus' Counter-Cultural Viewpoints	Cultural Viewpoints Might Say...
1. "whoever is forgiven much, loves much" (Luke 7:47)	
2. "he who is the least, shall be the greatest" (Luke 9:48)	
3. "don't fear those who can kill the body, fear Him who can destroy both body and soul" (Luke 12:4, 5)	
4. "I came, not to bring peace, but a sword" (Luke 12:49-53)	
5. "the first shall be last and the last shall be first" (Luke 13:30)	
6. "exalt yourself and be humbled, humble yourself and be exalted" (Luke 14:11)	
7. "he who is trusted with little will be trusted with much" (Luke 16:10)	

ACTIVITY #4: I'm a Christian School Teacher:
21 Questions to Get Me Started

---

1. *Do I intentionally plan to teach every unit and lesson Christianly? How will I accomplish this goal?*
2. *What is missing in any discipline or discussion that may be completed by Christian thought? Give an example.*
3. *How does supernatural revelation help us to "make sense" of what we confront in the natural world?*
4. *Does what I believe affect how I teach? How? Can I give an example?*
5. *How can I make my worldview more explicit in my discussion of ___? Give an example.*
6. *How often do I say my discipline is "sacred"? Explain what this means.*
7. *How often do I use "secular" to describe "non-Christian"? What should I say?*
8. *Do I show my students every day how God has displayed Himself in human language, grammar, writing, or reading? Can I give an example?*
9. *Do I point out the process of "seeing things" as sovereign and providential in the study of history? Can I give an example?*
10. *Do I point out the process of "seeing things" as error or truth in books, themes, or authors? Can I give an example?*
11. *Do we follow the lead of the latest educational directive or do we "set the plate" and "clear the path" for teaching Christianly?*
12. *What in our human experience drives us to find explanation or elucidation outside ourselves? What do we tell students when they ask questions about the unseen, miraculous, or incomprehensible?*
13. *What observations in creation can only be interpreted by The Creator?*

14. *What processes of life mentioned especially in the poetic books (i.e. evaporation, life cycles) establish baseline principles in all science?*
15. *Are there "accepted" Christian interpretations of life that need to be re-thought, re-tooled, re-explained in light of known, natural revelation? Can I give examples?*
16. *Have select Christian interpretations superceded the scope of Scriptural support? Are there any more Copernican revolutions "out there?" What should we change?*
17. *What markers of grace or pieces of truth are recorded in any thought, writing, dialectic, or drama? Give examples.*
18. *How does human desire show incompletion in what we long for? Explain.*
19. *How does The Pentateuch provide footings for law and policy for our own day? Give examples.*
20. *Why are primary colors limited? What does this teach about the visual arts in the Christian school?*
21. *What activities do we often participate in that reflect our humanness but we do not immediately connect to our spirit or our Lord (i.e. eating, hygiene, humor, etc.)?[9]*

ACTIVITY #5: A Self-Evaluation

Each Christian must willfully choose to grow in holiness and teach **wholeness.** *Answer the following questions individually.*

1. What objections might I bring to practicing biblical integration?
   - I have too much other material to cover.
   - I don't have enough time.
   - It's too hard.
   - My education degree had little or no biblical integration.
   - I don't care.
   - Other:

2. Before any subject, unit, lesson, lab, discussion, activity, lecture, or book is taught am I committing myself to asking the following questions:
   - How is what God says important for what I teach?
   - How does what I believe affect how I teach?
   - How is any topic completed by Christian thought?
   - How does salvation impact how I teach?

3. How can I incorporate these ideas into my lesson plans?

4. What five biblical principles do I communicate in each subject during the year? Do I plan or hope for these to occur?

5. How are these principles assessed in my lesson plan objectives, methods of instruction, and student evaluations?

6. How may other worldviews affect my teaching of ____?

7. How is the information or interpretation of my curriculum in harmony with the Christian worldview?

8. How do I "turn-things-on-their-head", thinking in Christian categories or paradigms?

9. What is the nature, quality, core, center, or essence of ____ as God intended it?

10. What makes what I teach different from anyone else in another school?

11. Am I claiming prayer before class, a verse-a-day, or Bible lesson as "biblical integration"? Why is this thinking wrong?

12. Do I refer to my school as "private" or "Christian"? Why might the definition matter?

ACTIVITY #6: Missions and Mottoes

Do We Practice What We Say We Believe?
Compare your school's mission and motto to the Christian philosophy of education. Answer two questions: (1) Is our present statement biblically correct? and (2) Are we doing what we say we do? If your school has no motto or it's time for a change, consider the examples below.

SAMPLE MISSION STATEMENT

The mission of ___ Christian School is to examine all of life from a biblical worldview. We are an institution who believes Jesus Christ is the core and completion of all our studies. Having been given the opportunity to think Christianly, students will provide real-world leadership in their God-gifted vocations.

EXAMPLE MOTTOS

Integrating Biblical Truth for Life.

Biblical Principles Unify All Truth.

Thinking Christianly, Contributing Vocationally.

Real World Leadership from an Other Worldly Perspective.

Constructing a Biblical Worldview, Biblically Constructive in the World

OUR PRESENT MISSION OR MOTTO:

COMPARISONS TO A CHRISTIAN SCHOOL PHILOSOPHY:

Chapter Six
The Meaning of Biblical Integration

My daughter began reading mysteries around the age of nine. They helped illuminate the biblical doctrine of sin. "What has to happen for a book to be a mystery?" I asked Chelsea. Her response came back, "Someone has to kill someone or steal something." "Right!" I asserted, "And what would the Bible call thievery or murder?" Matter-of-factly, the obvious reply, "Sin." "Exactly!" my face smiling, "Every time mystery writers write they explore the biblical doctrine of sin."

Dr. Seuss' *Horton Hears a Who* tells the wonderful primary level tale of Horton the elephant saving the society of *Who-ville* from extinction. The key theme running throughout the story, "a person's a person, no matter how small," calls to action anyone interested in preserving life. So important is the concept that crisis pregnancy centers sell the volume around the United States! But where did Dr. Seuss ultimately get the idea for his book? What is the core ideal? The only answer can be Genesis 1! Made in God's image, everyone has worth, value, and dignity. A Christian author may not state the doctrine, but it is a Christian concept!

Biblical integration brings to light the truth (or error) of any subject by interpreting it through Scripture. Biblical integration is concerned with *wholeness[1]*. Creation had intentional ideals set within itself by God (Proverbs 8:12-36). Sin fragmented human thought, life, universal connections, and the lot. The Christian's duty of redemption laid out by Jesus recaptures the fragments of

64

truth, excises the error, synthesizing, and recreating God's unique objective for His world.

Biblical Principles[2] Permeate Everything

"Permeation" suggests that the foundation of truth is God's and God accomplishes the unification of all truth. "Principled permeation" identifies errors and codifies instruction from books or ideas with tenets established in God's Word. Fragments of truth are acknowledged and made whole by God's revelation—the essence of coherence. Classification of truth, a system of rules, principles, or codes provides the framework necessary to compose rationale, scope and sequence, and lesson plan construction. Bible verses do not have to accompany every fraction written on the math board. What *is* important is to know why fractions can even exist by identifying that creational imprint from The Creator. The ideal biblical integration begins with the teacher's biblically informed mindset thinking about educational directives from God's point of view.

Consider the book *Frankenstein*. In her classic work Mary Shelley develops themes of fear, horror, and terror. It is the job of the Christian (and in the case of school, the Christian English teacher) to look at this piece of literature from a Christian point of view. Note the following examples:

Shelley wanted to "make the reader dread to look round, to curdle the blood, and quicken the beatings of the heart" by writing about the "mysterious fears of our nature and awaken[ing] thrilling horror." Humans scare easily because terror is real. Sudden movements may frighten us. When the unexpected happens, we scream. But the object of our fear is always something *different* than what we're used to. The monster in Frankenstein evokes a response from everyone he meets. Some cower. Others bristle. Many respond with a repugnance, aversion, or loathing. It is the *unusual* that people respond to most powerfully. It is good to be scared. Dread is an important biblical concept. Jeremiah states that the lack of terror of God was a problem for Israel (2:19). Quivering before God is the response of the writer in Psalm 119:120. God (Exodus 15:11), His Name (Deuteronomy 28:58), His deeds (Exodus 34:10), and His coming Day of Judgment (Isaiah 2:19; Joel 2:31) evokes a terrible trembling in people. The Egyptians who had seen enough of God's plagues responded properly to their dread (Exodus 9:20). In fact, by fearing God there is no need to fear anything or anyone else (Isaiah 8:12-13).[3]

In Christian homes and schools, everything should be based on a biblical worldview. Since Christians are in the course of growing in Christ, distinctive thinking is a continuous and often arduous development. We live in a world encumbered by an anti-Christian bias (2 Corinthians 4:4; 11:1-15; 1 John 4:1-6). So the individual Christian must bring a biblical thought process to bear on people, policy, and practice. This biblical thought process in not natural, it requires a proactive renewing of the mind on the part of believers (Romans 12:1-2).

What Biblical Integration *Is Not*

It is essential to personally understand the essence or core idea of books, concepts, or subjects areas for Biblical integration to be practiced. However, the definition of biblical integration is not up for discussion. It cannot mean one thing to one person and another to someone else.[4] "We do it this way at our school" or "I do it this way in my classroom" is a subjective analysis. Before continuing to develop how to practice biblical integration it is helpful to delineate what it is *not*. Often, explaining the negative brings more light to bear on the positive.

*Biblical Integration is **not** Illustration*

Studying the slope of a line in geometry, the math teacher opened his Bible to a pre-marked spot in Joshua 15:8 reading Judah's allotment of land that ran "along the southern slope of the Jebusite city." Thinking that biblical integration had taken place, the math class was free to move on to board work. A second grade teacher was communicating math facts by using blocks. "Four blocks plus five blocks equals nine blocks. Put them together and we have towers of blocks." It was later suggested by an outside observer that the class had missed a wonderful opportunity to see biblical integration at work. When asked what that might be the observer enthused, "Why, The Tower of Babel, of course!" Simply finding similar word connections was considered to be biblical integration. In another case, a consultant was asked for help in doing biblical integration in math. The educator drew a triangle. "This is the mathematical basis for The Trinity" was his conclusion. Symbols typified the biblical basis of math in his view.

Finding connective notions in the Bible that match terms in the lesson is *not* biblical integration. The problem with illustration or metaphor is that anything can be employed as illustration.[5] The Bible is then used as a talisman, a good luck charm.[6] "If I quote or allude to a Bible verse, I have fulfilled my duty as a Christian school teacher," some would erroneously conclude. Studying biological truths about blood, for instance, should not lead the science class to hear "Just as we need blood for life, so we need Jesus' blood for new life."[7] When Hebrews 6:14 says, "We have an anchor for our hope," biblical integration *is not* "plants are anchored by their roots just as we have an anchor for our soul."

Biblical Integration is *not* Character Quality Instruction

In the 1990's *Character Counts* instruction was instituted in government schools and was premised upon *The Six Pillars*—vague notions of moral codes. It was made clear throughout community school systems that these pillars had no connection to any specific religious beliefs. While character development has been crucial in establishing affective changes in the lives of students, it is impossible to construct character-based education apart from the groundwork of the Christian worldview. The obvious question students will ask is, "Who says?" On what basis should a pupil be trustworthy or kind? If a player elbows his opponent under the basket, gets the rebound, scores, and wins the game, isn't that what it's all about? Only the Old and New Testaments argue for a transcendent source of truth claims that give character development a foundation.

But even if *Character Counts* didn't have a philosophical base to stand on, isn't it *still* teaching good character? Herein is the problem for the Christian school. Even if Bible verses are attached to character qualities, the same ideas are being taught down the street at the local school. What makes the Christian school distinctive? If Johnny is taught to be responsible in every school the only real difference is the cost of tuition. For instance, in some communities Christian teachers have a high profile and are a strong influence in government schools. And conservative segments of the country often mirror a Judeo-Christian ethic in their policy and practice. Character instruction is part and parcel of some neighborhoods in every state. The Christian school cannot be distinctive in its instruction of all subjects if what is meant by biblical integration is only character quality precepts. There must be something different and all permeating.

Biblical Integration is *not* Spiritualization

"Our verse for the day is on the board, let's all say it

68

together." "In our Bible lesson today we want to study Joshua." "Class, we need to put God first in our lives." Phrases like these are uttered in Christian schools across the globe. They do not, however, put subjects in a biblical frame. They are merely segments of Christian truth dropped in and around curricula. They create a dichotomy of spiritual and secular by relegating all things Christian to trite phrases and generalized goodness. But, as has been clearly seen, there is no dichotomy between molecular structure and Messiah's rule over His world. Personal piety is important. Pietism, on the other hand, leads people toward preoccupation with an individualized salvation and away from responsibility to the whole world. Devotion is Christian dedication. Devotionals, conversely, divide biblical truth from real world interaction. Living in a world that acknowledges spiritual things, much more needs to be done to make education characteristically Christian. Prayer before class, Bible reading, chapel, or study of Scripture in Christian schools may be good, but does not make a school "Christian."

*Biblical Integration is **not** Transmission*

Promotional materials for some Christian schools declare, "We feature top academics, discipline, and a college preparation atmosphere." And though this may draw a greater amount of students, the obvious question remains, "What makes that Christian?" With increased societal pressure on test scores and academic standing, some Christian institutions are augmenting their abilities in these arenas. And, as has been said before, there is nothing wrong with a desire for a high level of competency, rigor, and discipline in studies. But if Christian academies are only interested in beating other schools at their own game, then the battle has already been lost. Separating academics from the meticulousness of understanding specific subjects permeated by biblical truth raises the stature of schools in the eyes of community members without providing deliberative Christian distinction.

Biblical Integration is *not* Correlation

Finding citations about *'numbers'* in the Bible for math class only tells us that the concept of *'number'* existed and was utilized in ancient culture. Finding prepositional phrases in the Psalms becomes the pedantic search for grammar within the guise of using the Bible. This approach raises potentially divisive problems in understanding Scripture. For example, because the Bible says God sent His people to war in the Old Testament does not directly give Christians the basis for going to war today. Automatic parallels between the text of Scripture and the social studies text could prove problematic. Furthermore, what if the Bible does not speak to a certain topic? Perhaps nuclear power is addressed in a class. God's Word was written prior to a human knowledge of nuclear fission. What is the teacher to do if God said nothing specific on the subject? Correlation runs into problems because connections to a concept cannot explain the essence, role, or operation of a person, place, or thing.

Biblical Integration is *not* Application

"Let's demonstrate being 'doers of The Word' through this week's service project." "You can discuss the ethical implications of in vitro fertilization in Bible class." "Music theory is one thing, singing spiritual songs to God in chapel is another." Obviously the problem remains one of detachment if biblical truth applies to life only in certain circumstances, at certain points in the school calendar. Subject matter is disconnected from foundational, infusive scriptural insight into the operation of God's world. Service projects, Bible classes, and chapels could be important components in Christian school education, but these by themselves do not make education *Christian*.

70

Biblical Integration is **not** Evangelization

"I'm glad that I'm in a Christian school so I can share my testimony of Jesus with my students." Depending on the mission of any given school, apologetic witness may well be the basis for communication of Christian truth.[8]   For many, however, apologetics does not cross the mind of Christian school instructors who make the above-mentioned assertion. Some people with a Christian worldview do not use their doctrine much past the need for someone's individual salvation. Understanding the whole world and all of life from God's perspective is not intended. Once again, subject matter is taught the same way any non-Christian might teach it. Indeed, leading children to the cross initiates life change. But the life-changing message of Jesus' death, burial, and resurrection must saturate every corner of a person, transforming the mind, engaging God's world, and bringing every thought captive to Christ.

Biblical Integration is **not** Personification

"Modeling the Christian life in the classroom is my best contribution in my Christian school." It may be. Discipleship and mentoring are the processes of encouraging godliness in the next generation of Christian young people. Yet again, the lack of interaction with Christian truth in every area of the curriculum curtails any distinction the Christian school might address. Many would argue persuasively that the collective encouragement of home, youth group, Bible studies, prayer cells, Christian music, books, movies, and periodicals is all a teenager needs for growth in Christ. So apart from being added to the list, a Christian school finds itself as just another tool to help *keep kids Christian*.

It should be said that Christian institutions are often aligned within the framework of a complimentary mission: the triangular involvement of church, home, and school.[9] While the mission does not change, often, neither does the mind of the Christian

71

school student. They are left with the distinct impression that if they grow up to be mathematicians, chemists, plumbers, financial consultants, coaches, teachers, or sanitation workers, their life is segmented into *what they do for a living* versus *how they live as Christians*. Instead, Christian discipleship should be a discipleship of the mind. Regeneration should renovate the boardroom, schoolroom, bedroom, and every-room. Suzie should leave the Christian school knowing that God's principles sustain math as creation's language, chemistry as purposed properties, finances as God-owned and given, coaching as reclaiming the Hebraic view of the whole person, teaching as integrating biblical truth for life, and sanitation as applied Levitical law protecting people from disease, to name a few.

What Biblical Integration *Is*

The economics class begins the semester by discovering how wealth is created. Entrepreneurial enterprise, it is taught, must be framed by an outside source of law to maintain ethical boundaries. Within the rule of transcendent law, God's image bearers live out their freedom, individuality, and creativity to craft goods and services that sustain God's creation.

Fourth graders learning about the U.S. Constitution come across the *checks and balances* that limit power within government. The teacher explains that Lord Acton's principle, "power corrupts and absolute power corrupts absolutely," is premised upon the biblical doctrine of sin. Since it's not wise to place power within the hands of one or two, our government's power is divided among the executive, legislative, judicial branches. The students also learn that human sinfulness is pervasive in all people and that this biblical doctrine influenced the founding principles of constitutionalism.

Eighth graders are asked to examine and comment on George Orwell's *Animal Farm*. Through reading, interpretation, and discussion students discover that one dictatorship is just as bad as another. The warnings are clear: evil spreads when good people do nothing.

Whatever the class, subject, discussion, book, or idea, **biblical principles should permeate everything.** *Wholeness. Synthesis. Completion.* Words such as these carry the focus of true Christian education. Teachers need to recover God-centered thought patterns that invigorate every discipline. James Orr proclaimed this veracity at the end of the 19th century:

> No duty is more imperative on the Christian teacher than that of showing that instead of Christianity being simply one theory among the rest, it is really the higher truth which is the synthesis and completion of all the others; that view which, rejecting the error, takes up the vitalizing (sic) elements in all other systems and religions, and unites them into a living organism, with Christ as head.[10]

The following six questions are important for helping Christian teachers to realize and understand exactly what Biblical Integration *is*.

1. What Was God's Intention in Genesis 1 and 2?

Before sin corrupted God's creation everything was as He intended. Everything was good. As has been said previously, it is the Christian's responsibility to reclaim everything and make it good again. Genesis 1 and 2 are the basis for this reclamation because they show us what God intended. God's good intention is echoed in a marvelous hymn that demonstrates God's Lordship over all of His creation and creation's response:

Earth and all stars, loud rushing planets,
Sing to the Lord a new song!
O victory, loud shouting army,
Sing to the Lord a new song!
Hail, wind, and rain, loud blowing snowstorms,
Sing to the Lord a new song!
Flowers and trees, loud rustling dry leaves,
Sing to the Lord a new song!
Trumpet and pipes, loud clashing cymbals,
Sing to the Lord a new song!
Harp, lute, and lyre, loud humming cellos,
Sing to the Lord a new song!
Engines and steel, loud pounding hammers,
Sing to the Lord a new song!
Limestone and beams, loud building workers,
Sing to the Lord a new song!
Classrooms and labs, loud boiling test tubes,
Sing to the Lord a new song!
Athlete and band, loud cheering people,
Sing to the Lord a new song!
Knowledge and truth, loud sounding wisdom,
Sing to the Lord a new song!
Daughter and son, loud praying members,
Sing to the Lord a new song![11]

So when the art teacher organizes her classes and premises any aesthetic enterprise upon the proposition in Genesis 2:9, "God made trees...that were pleasing to the eye and good for food," that is biblical integration. The fruit of God's world is not only for consumption, but for visual enjoyment, also. Art is not for art's sake, but for His sake.

Consider another example in which fourth graders discuss why policemen are important. The teacher explains God's aim: law and order comes from moral order based upon creation order.

74

Similarly, the high school political science class contrasts the biblical model with Jean-Jacques Rousseau's *The Social Contract*: humans are basically good and are made better through education plus political change. As elementary students become teenagers they begin to see that autonomous human law leads to tyranny and creation order produces an opportunity for republics based on God's law.

Using a concordance to study the attributes of water in the Bible could help to elucidate the origin, function, and properties of water if Scripture speaks directly to these things. For instance, Psalm 104 details the creation of water in clouds (v. 3) and on earth (v. 6). Boundaries, such as seashores, are established (vv. 7-9). Underground springs (v. 10) and rainfall (v. 13) provide refreshment. Both landmasses and humanity benefit from the life giving qualities of water (vv. 11-18). Furthermore, God regulates water (Leviticus 26:4 and Deuteronomy 28:12). His concerns include river flow (Numbers 24:6) and wells (Genesis 16:14). Disobedient human conduct can inhibit water's essential life giving qualities (cf. Leviticus 26:19 or Amos 4:7). In general, God is the source, sustainer, and sovereign ruler (cf. Exodus 15:1-18) of water.[12]

2. How has Sin Distorted the Topic of Study?

The Fall fragmented human thinking. It is imperative for the Christian to understand that sin corrupts all of life, because this points to the need for reclaiming everything for God. "Pure" cannot be used as a description of anything since Genesis 3. Subjects such as math, science, and grammar must be acknowledged as damaged goods. Consider the following statement of belief for the Christian school grammar class:

Grammatical Proposition:
Whereas, sin has corrupted every realm of earth's existence; and because language is susceptible to

sin's effects; and because, without grammatical rules, language would be incoherent and chaotic; and because rules are a reflection of The Divine Order throughout creation; and because language is inexorably tied to grammar's function; and because doctrine is bound to the precision of language; and because false teaching influences doctrine; and because word choice matters in biblical instruction;[13] Let it be known, that the study of grammar is imperative to halt the corrosive effects of sin upon our thought processes and the undermining of the communication of True Truth in life and doctrine (2 Peter 3:15-18; 2 John 4; 3 John 3, 4).

Grading is susceptible to corruption—even in objective testing. Teachers may construct poorly worded tests, not consider the ability level of the class, or worse, create a document with the mindset of, "I'll show *them!*" Understanding our human propensity toward wrong behavior, teachers should adopt and communicate the acrostic "C.I.A.": evaluation is for correction[14], improvement[15], and accountability[16]. Objectivity in grading can be improved if everyone remembers the effects of sin's disruption.

Books and authors must be critiqued to expose distorted teaching. Jack London's *Call of the Wild* is an evolutionary treatise. Jack was an atheist as well as a Marxist-Leninist. The theme of the book is "red in tooth and claw," "it's a dog-eat-dog world," and "the strong survive." Read in the Christian school classroom London's prose must come under the scrutiny of Scripture to show it's faulty view of the world.

3. How Can the Subject be Repaired by Christian Thought?

The idea that salvation has made everything redeemable must be communicated otherwise there's no basis for redemption.

76

Biblical principles reconcile everything that God has made by the simple fact that God deems them important.

Math and its applications in engineering, the sciences, or business are regulated by the overarching principle of God's immutability: He does not change (Malachi 3:6). Thus math does not change. As a case in point, estimation works because mathematical patterns are predictable. Predictability finds its source in the dependable, faithful Creator. Hence, bridges and buildings are constructed, quantitative and qualitative studies are statistically analyzed, and bookkeeping methods are premised upon unmoving creational principles. Since sin has shattered the unity of the world, the world is in need of external, unwavering standards of impartiality. Correcting daily math problems, spelling mistakes, and picking up after ourselves mirrors the Christian teaching of redemption.

At recess an argument may break out over fairness about a four square game. The teacher, having earlier discussed how our sinful nature can make a game degenerate into "winners versus losers" or a "head-trip" for someone's ego, prods her students to identify principles that underscore regenerative elements by asking, "How can we think Christianly about playing games?" Individualized events, such as the four square contest, stipulate sportsmanship. Competition forces discipline and hones skills. Developing these qualities evidences a Christian commitment to hard work (Romans 12:3-8). Some answers for group games may include emphasis on cooperation and teamwork or the fact that all great teams work together. We spend our lives working *with* people (1 Corinthians 12; Ephesians 4:1-6).

4. How Do Worldviews Produce World Changers?

Beliefs fashion the life and thinking of everyone: author, historian, journalist, movie producer, playwright, poet, scientist, or sociologist. Peoples' beliefs affect what they produce. Knowing the background of individuals of note in any discipline will shed light on their personal directions and contributions. At times, shifts in philosophy change policy and opinion about righteousness or evil. Identifying the perspectives of everyone from astronomers to zoologists is imperative so that students see how thought precedes and prompts action.

Examples of Christians and their positive influences in the world are voluminous. Ocean shipping lanes are dependant upon ocean currents, which were first discovered by Matthew Maury. Inspired by the phrase in Psalm 8:8 "paths of the seas" Maury's *Physical Geography of the Sea* accentuated the belief that scientific statements in the Bible were accurate.[17] Katherine Patterson's books are marked with obvious connections to biblical truth. *Jacob Have I Loved* shows that the goodness of God in one's life often follows a trail of pain. Grimms' Fairy Tales are actually infused with biblical faith that helps create a moral base for thinking.[18] Children's books like *Squanto and the Miracle of Thanksgiving*[19] correct historic inaccuracies in popular curriculum. Native Americans like Pocohontas and Sacagawea demonstrate the life changing power of Jesus' gospel in the lives of those who create positive interconnections between people groups.

On the other hand there are examples of unbelieving influences that can be examined Christianly. G. H. Hardy in *A Mathematician's Apology* argued that math was a pure demonstration of truth, goodness, and beauty even though applied math can be used to create war machines. Hardy's life, with mathematics as his sole interest, ended in attempted suicide, despair, and sadness because he could no longer *do* math.[20] Film director Ingmar Bergman explains in his autobiography, *The Magic Lantern,* that his austere, harsh father—a pastor—drove him from The Church. He spent the rest of his life seeking purpose through the medium of film. The humanistic search for meaning infected his most famous devotee, Woody Allen. D. Bruce Lockerbie exposes the backgrounds and beliefs of unbelieving

78

eighteenth and nineteenth century British and American authors in *Dismissing God.* The authorial disbelief of some like Ernest Hemingway, Friedrich Nietzsche, or Jean-Paul Sartre spiraled into nihilism until only a void of truth remained.[21] And even Christians often accept Maslow's hierarchies as a tool for understanding educational psychology. Anti-supernaturalism, however, guided the self-actualization approach leading Maslow to the conclusion that religious people could not even achieve the highest level of his hierarchy.

5. What Makes our School Distinctively Christian?

Why should we share, help, or be polite? Since our authority comes from God, manners are not a result of "because I said so" but because God said so. It is essential to explain that adults are not the final authority—God is. Only God can answer the "why" question because He is the answer to "Who says?"

But at times Christians merely "baptize" a pagan concept with a Bible verse, "cleansing" it for use in the classroom. Sometimes Christian schoolteachers adopt practices that actually run counter to Scriptural teaching. Rewards are a case in point. B. F. Skinner modeled behavioralism as the change agent for pupils. Habitual responses are awarded merit creating certain human performance. But the Bible says intrinsic (internal) worth should be valued over extrinsic (external) incentive. The "prize box" should be replaced by encouraging words (Proverbs 12:8; 14:34; 27:21). Rewards often take place well after the act, in some cases not until eternity (cf. 2 Timothy 4:8). Rewards are good relationships with God (Proverbs 8:35; 11:20; 12:2, 22) and others (Proverbs 3:3-4; 11:16; 22:1). Rewards are intangible benefits: wisdom (Proverbs 8:35; 9:12), faithfulness (Proverbs 14:22), and freedom (Proverbs 11:21). Rewards are not bribes (Proverbs 17:8; 29:4); bribes pervert justice (Proverbs 17:23). Rewards are not necessarily immediate. A "long life" (Proverbs 10:27:12:28) or a

79

"good reputation" (Proverbs 10:7; 12:8; 13:15; 19:11) is extended over many years. Rewards are not necessarily visible such as in a person's grace (Proverbs 1:9; 21:21) or security (Proverbs 10:9; 14:26). Wealth and prosperity (Proverbs 3:2; 8:18, 22:1; 10:22, etc.) are developed over a long period of time and are based upon someone's internalized way of life, not a response to stimuli.

Why we teach anything forms the framework of thinking for anyone. If everyone integrates belief, they begin, consciously or unconsciously, with an approach to a course. An imperative, invaluable process of distinctively Christian teaching would be the development of one's course philosophy[22]. Elementary teachers could write a paragraph on how being a Christian maps the direction of the class. Junior and senior high teachers could articulate their courses Christianly, further explaining major units of study. In the following example, note how basic doctrinal teaching surrounds and binds the study of history. Christian truth must form the foundation, unification, and permeation of Christian school courses or classes.

The Christian Philosophy of History

History begins in eternity. God's activity within this life establishes human destiny in the afterlife. Human history is premised upon five major attributes of God.

1. <u>God is eternal.</u> The temporal, finite world exists because there is One who is "from everlasting to everlasting" (Psalm 90:2), whose "dominion is eternal" (Daniel 4:34, 35), and who works within time for human benefit (Psalm 31:15; 39:4-7).
2. <u>God is creator.</u> All things, including time, were made by and for Himself (Genesis 1:1; Romans 11:33-36; Colossians 1:15-17).

3. God foreordains. The plan of God for His world was "declared from the distant past" (Isaiah 45:21; 46:9-11; Ephesians 1:9-11).
4. God is Providential. He personally oversees and is actively involved with all people, places, and events (Genesis 50:20; James 4:14-17). He controls all events. There are no accidents or coincidences. Luck, destiny, and chance do not contribute to any earthly event (Acts 2:23; 4:27, 28; 17:26).
5. God is sovereign. The absolute rule of earth is God's alone. His kingship is all inclusive of authority, ownership, and control. (Job 12:23; Psalm 22:28; 50:9-12)

6. How can Christian Schools be a Work in Process?

Understanding that sanctification in Christ is at the heart of integration leads one to realize that we as humans can never be finished with integration. Just as our maturation in Christ, our need to know Him more fully, is never finished until the moment of glorification, so our need as Christian's to reclaim the world from sin is never finished until that moment. Understanding all things through Christ is a matter of continual growth. Because God has told us that He is infinite and we are finite, we know that we can never know all things. But He has also told us to strive for what we can know—and that striving can never be complete because we will never be infinite. John Milton suggested in *On Education* that ours was the responsibility of "repair[ing] the ruins of our first parents by regaining to know God aright..."[23] Increasing our knowledge of God expands our understanding of His view of the world.

"Every time I open a book I discover how much I don't know." Acknowledging this famous dictum is similar to discovering more about God and His creation. The work is never

81

done. An important principle of Scripture is "the infinite and the finite" (Genesis 1; Job 38-42; Romans 11:33-36). We can never see or know *every*thing. Thus, before coming to conclusions on some matters, it may be better to wait and see if other information will shed new light. We must accept God's illumination of the Scriptures, realizing that our sinfulness hinders our reception of His Word. Every passage is alive, relevant, and the direct instruction of God. Since discovery is continuous for finite minds in a finite universe, it is best to recognize and stand in awe of the Infinite Creator.

The Scriptural tenet of the finite and the infinite, of learning and what is to be learned, is directly tied to how we practice biblical integration. It also has integrative application to such things as the exploration and investigation in all areas of learning (i.e., genetic links to behavior; human health factors; archaeology; space probes; etc.). If we are always learning, then the latest studies may not be definitive. The long road of research suggests anything but a quick fix. The historical novel *Isaac's Storm* tells a story to that effect. In 1900 a hurricane hit Galveston, Texas. Ultimately, upwards of 10,000 lives were lost. At the time, meteorology was considered to be an exact science and human pride produced a false sense of security—no one thought a hurricane would hit Galveston.

At times, the answers have been right there all along and we just cannot see them without going the long way around. For instance, who would have ever thought that pigment had power? [24] Vitamins in pill form are no substitute for the life giving, disease restricting blue in blueberries, red in strawberries, orange in carrots, and even the brown in chocolate. Color is attractive to the eye and good for the body. Vegetable and fruit pigments contain antioxidants, which have anti-aging and anti-inflammatory properties, reducing the risk of disease. God's creation is replete with easily recognizable nutrition, something the process of science continues to uncover.

Growing a Christian faculty is also a process. Wheaton Academy, a large Christian high school in West Chicago, Illinois, uses advertisements for teachers are second to none. "Looking for Christian teachers who will teach worldviewishly, this Christian secondary school models what it means to secure Christian thought in all subject areas." Jon Keith, the principal at Wheaton Academy, wants instructors who will "look at all of life through the lens of scripture while modeling a Biblical worldview that guides their thoughts, words and deeds."[25] The Academy has also initiated a plan to guarantee biblical integration within a process of continuing education for its teachers. Realizing that teachers are always learning is the basis for what the Academy calls its "living curriculum."

Showing that Christian schools should be a work in process, the following outline ascertains performance plans for faculty and their curricula:

A. Hiring Teachers who Think and Teach Christianly

- Find colleges that train education students in biblical integration.
- Commit to biblical integration first, state certification second.
- Provide personal bible study training to help teachers develop a truly Christian worldview that pervades their lives and teaching.

B. Training Teachers to Think and Teach Christianly

Instructional requirements should include:

- Daily reinforcement in and encouragement of biblical integration (e.g. meetings, informal dialogue, and lesson plans)

83

- Weekly coaching in biblical integration by administration and peers (e.g. classroom observations and one-on-one scheduled interaction)
- Monthly opportunities to develop biblical principles in academic areas (e.g. reading, in-services, seminars, round-table forums, and continuing education courses)
- Yearly interaction with other Christian educators through institutes in geographical proximity to the school (e.g. local colleges, retreats, and conventions)
- Yearly occasions to write or speak to colleagues in areas of expertise for the benefit of the Christian school movement
- Yearly mentoring for Christian college, teacher-training programs
- Yearly partnerships with Christian universities which prepare Christian teachers to teach Christianly providing the school with a resource for future instructors.

C. Writing Curriculum that Discovers Biblical Truth in Each Discipline

Curricular requirements should include:

- Writing the biblical philosophy of academic areas (e.g. **why** a subject is important).
- Writing the biblical, educational objectives (e.g. **how** the subject should be taught).

Steps such as these will guide the growth of a model Christian school. Visioning continual growth for Christian education is dependent upon institutions dedicated to (1) the hiring and instructing of Christian school teachers to think and teach Christianly in every subject area, (2) communicating the Christian worldview to every student for whatever vocation they are gifted, and (3) perpetuating the process of Christian teacher and curricula development.[26]

Activity #7: Thoughts, Suggestions, and Possibilities
Interact with some or all of the questions below,
considering the consequences for the individual and institution.

Personal Assessment
How can we train our minds to think Christianly about everything?
Curriculum Revision
How does our shift in thinking about curriculum mirror our commitment for training our students to apply the biblical worldview in everything?
The Reformation of Syllabi
How can we introduce students to studies outside our fields that would begin to demonstrate a wholistic approach to the Christian life?
An Emphasis on Biblical Theology
How can we maintain a commitment to inductive Bible study whose application is taught throughout the curriculum?
Synthesis Coupled with Analysis
How is the tension to know detail and overview maintained in our teaching so that students begin to recognize the completion of all thought in Christ?
Teaching Lifelong Learners
How are we training students to develop frameworks and rubrics to think and live differently than their pagan counterparts?
Restructuring Classroom Space
How can we reorganize our classrooms so that we encourage interaction between departments for expanding our integrative theological, pedagogical, and practical horizons?
Faculty and Departmental Meetings
How can we include cross-disciplinary discussions over biblical integration on a monthly basis?
Credentialing
How can we encourage faculty to be both specialists and generalists? How would this encourage biblical integration?
Faculty Hiring and Training
How do we encourage our instructors to think integratively all the time?

Chapter 7
The Model of Biblical Integration

We are to view all of life through the "lens" of Scripture. Biblical integration means to recapture the fragments of truth scattered by sin into a whole—God's perspective on the world. Multiple visual examples of this are diagrammed on the following pages. Each chart is designed for a unique aspect of life. But notice how each process moves from left to right, beginning with God's thoughts about His world and we interpret our teaching from his perspective. Also realize that principles in one area may well affect other areas of life. Many principles from diagrams #14-19, for instance, could be incorporated into a computer class as principles guiding repetition, long-term accomplishment, hard work, and strategizing. Mathematics students responsible to master rote concepts such as times tables could also be encouraged by the precepts modeled here: memory work leads to reinforcement, routine, incremental gain, satisfaction, and the idea that if *you-don't-use-it-you'll-lose-it* mentality.

Diagram #7 The Model for Practicing Biblical Integration

THE MODEL OF BIBLICAL INTEGRATION

How is the idea completed by Christian thought? As believers in Jesus as Lord, we see the world differently than others. We view all of life through the "lens" of Scripture. Biblical integration recaptures the fragments of truth scattered by sin into a whole-God's perspective on the world. The Christian teacher then lives out a change of knowledge, attitude, and lifestyle.

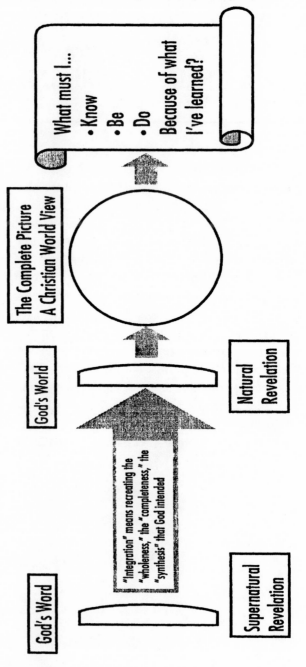

The Complete Picture
A Christian World View

What must I...
• Know
• Be
• Do
Because of what
I've learned?

God's World

Natural
Revelation

God's Word

Supernatural
Revelation

"Integration" means recreating the "wholeness," the "completeness," the "synthesis" that God intended

Diagram #8 The Pictorial Model of Biblical Integration

The following outline could function as the basis for lesson plan development.
Since most teachers are given certain curricula to teach they might begin with
asking "What biblical passage/principle permeates what I'm teaching?"

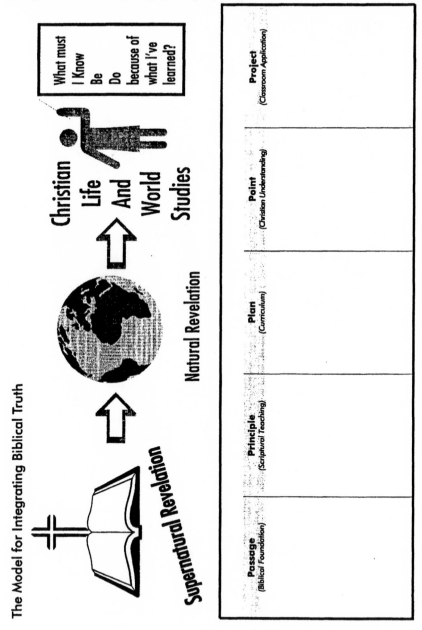

Diagram #9 Integrating Biblical Truth in Physical Education

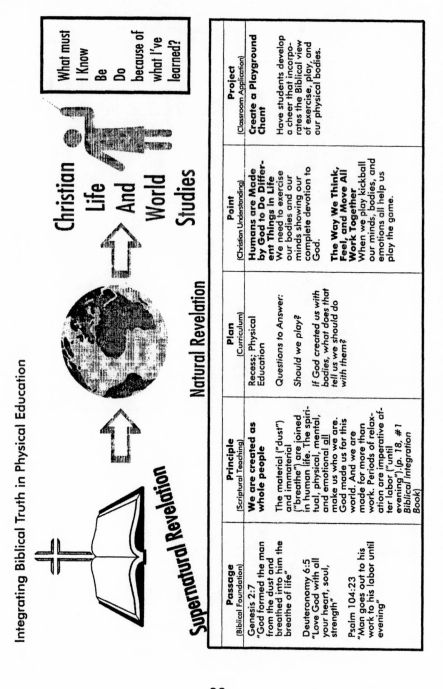

Integrating Biblical Truth in Physical Education

What must
I Know
Be
Do
because of
what I've
learned?

Supernatural Revelation

Natural Revelation

Christian Life And World Studies

Passage (Biblical Foundation)	Principle (Scriptural Teaching)	Plan (Curriculum)	Point (Christian Understanding)	Project (Classroom Application)
Genesis 2:7 "God formed the man from the dust and breathed into him the breathe of life" Deuteronomy 6:5 "Love God with all your heart, soul, strength" Psalm 104:23 "Man goes out to his work to his labor until evening"	We are created as whole people The material ("dust") and immaterial ("breathe") are joined in human life. The spiritual, physical, mental, and emotional all make us who we are. God made us for this world. And we are made for more than work. Periods of relaxation are imperative after labor ("until evening"). (p. 18, #1 Biblical Integration Book)	Recess; Physical Education Questions to Answer: Should we play? If God created us with bodies, what does that tell us we should do with them?	Humans are Made by God to Do Different Things in Life We need to exercise our bodies and our minds showing our complete devotion to God. The Way We Think, Feel, and Move All Work Together When we play kickball our minds, bodies, and emotions all help us play the game.	Create a Playground Chant Have students develop a cheer that incorporates the Biblical view of exercise, play, and our physical bodies.

Diagram #10 Integrating Biblical Truth in Recreation

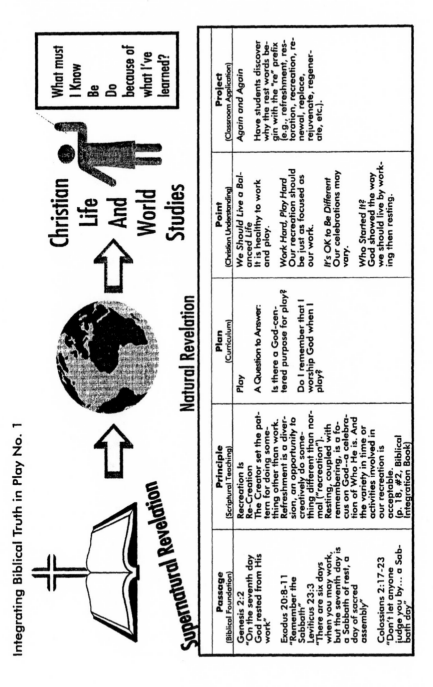

Integrating Biblical Truth in Play No. 1

Supernatural Revelation → Natural Revelation → Christian Life And World Studies

What must
I Know
Be
Do
because of what I've learned?

Passage (Biblical Foundation)	Principle (Scriptural Teaching)	Plan (Curriculum)	Point (Christian Understanding)	Project (Classroom Application)
Genesis 2:2 "On the seventh day God rested from His work" Exodus 20:8-11 "Remember the Sabbath" Leviticus 23:3 "There are six days when you may work, but the seventh day is a Sabbath of rest, a day of sacred assembly" Colossians 2:17-23 "Don't let anyone judge you by... a Sabbath day"	Recreation Is Re-Creation The Creator set the pattern for doing something other than work. Refreshment is a diversion, an opportunity to creatively do something different than normal ("recreation"). Resting, coupled with remembering, is a focus on God--a celebration of Who He is. And the variety in time or activities involved in our recreation is acceptable. (p. 18, #2, Biblical Integration Book)	Play A Question to Answer: Is there a God-centered purpose for play? Do I remember that I worship God when I play?	We Should Live a Balanced Life It is healthy to work and play. Work Hard, Play Hard Our recreation should be just as focused as our work. It's OK to Be Different Our celebrations may vary. Who Started It? God showed the way we should live by working then resting.	Again and Again Have students discover why the rest words begin with the "re" prefix (e.g.,, refreshment, restoration, recreation, renewal, replace, rejuvenate, regenerate, etc.).

Diagram #11 Integrating Biblical Truth in Play

Integrating Biblical Truth in Play No. 2

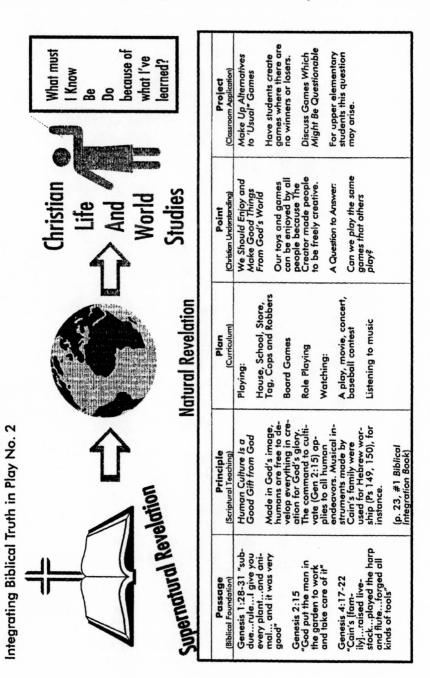

Supernatural Revelation

Natural Revelation

Christian Life And World Studies

What must
I Know
Be
Do
because of
what I've
learned?

Passage (Biblical Foundation)	Principle (Scriptural Teaching)	Plan (Curriculum)	Point (Christian Understanding)	Project (Classroom Application)
Genesis 1:28-31 "subdue...rule...I give you every plant...and animal... and it was very good"	Human Culture Is a Good Gift from God	Playing:	We Should Enjoy and Make Good Things From God's World	Make Up Alternatives to "Usual" Games
Genesis 2:15 "God put the man in the garden to work and take care of it"	Made in God's image, humans are free to develop everything in creation for God's glory. The command to cultivate (Gen 2:15) applies to all human endeavors. Musical instruments made by Cain's family were used for Hebrew worship (Ps 149, 150), for instance.	House, School, Store, Tag, Cops and Robbers

Board Games

Role Playing

Watching: | Our toys and games can be enjoyed by all people because The Creator made people to be freely creative.

A Question to Answer: | Have students create games where there are no winners or losers.

Discuss Games Which Might Be Questionable |
| Genesis 4:17-22 "Cain's [family]...raised livestock...played the harp and flute...forged all kinds of tools" | (p. 23, #1 Biblical Integration Book) | A play, movie, concert, baseball contest

Listening to music | Can we play the same games that others play? | For upper elementary students this question may arise. |

Diagram #12 Integrating Biblical Truth in Work Before Play

Integrating Biblical Truth in Play No. 3

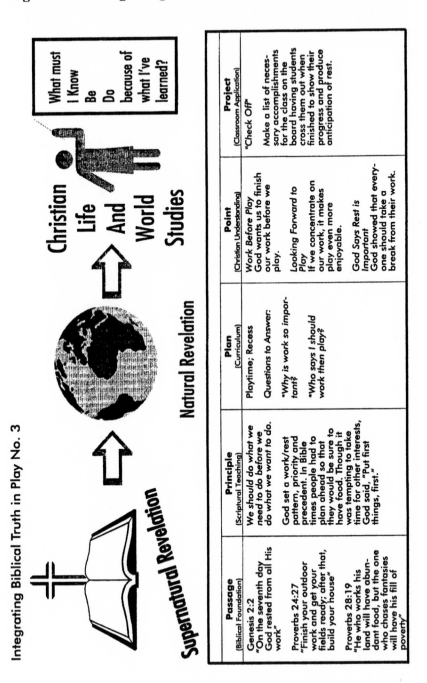

What must
I Know
Be
Do
because of
what I've
learned?

Christian
Life
And
World
Studies

Natural Revelation

Supernatural Revelation

Passage (Biblical Foundation)	Principle (Scriptural Teaching)	Plan (Curriculum)	Point (Christian Understanding)	Project (Classroom Application)
Genesis 2:2 "On the seventh day God rested from all His work"	We should do what we need to do before we do what we want to do. God set a work/rest pattern, priority and precedent. In Bible times people had to plan ahead so that they would be sure to have food. Though it was tempting to take time for other interests, God said, "Put first things, first."	Playtime; Recess Questions to Answer: *Why is work so important? *Who says I should work then play?	Work Before Play God wants us to finish our work before we play. Looking Forward to Play If we concentrate on our work, it makes play even more enjoyable. God Says Rest is Important God showed that everyone should take a break from their work.	"Check Off" Make a list of necessary accomplishments for the class on the board having students cross them out when finished to show their progress and produce anticipation of rest.
Proverbs 24:27 "Finish your outdoor work and get your fields ready; after that, build your house"				
Proverbs 28:19 "He who works his land will have abundant food, but the one who chases fantasies will have his fill of poverty"				

Diagram #13 Integrating Biblical Truth in Enjoying Life

Integrating Biblical Truth in Play No. 4

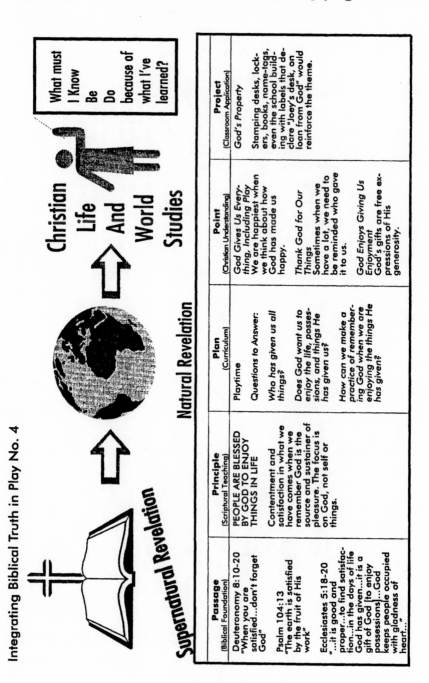

Supernatural Revelation

Natural Revelation

Christian
Life
And
World
Studies

What must
I Know
Be
Do
because of
what I've
learned?

Passage (Biblical Foundation)	Principle (Scriptural Teaching)	Plan (Curriculum)	Point (Christian Understanding)	Project (Classroom Application)
Deuteronomy 8:10-20 "When you are satisfied....don't forget God" Psalm 104:13 "The earth is satisfied by the fruit of His work" Ecclesiastes 5:18-20 "...it is good and proper...to find satisfaction...in the days of life God has given...it is a gift of God [to enjoy possessions]....God keeps people occupied with gladness of heart..."	PEOPLE ARE BLESSED BY GOD TO ENJOY THINGS IN LIFE Contentment and satisfaction in what we have comes when we remember God is the source and sustainer of pleasure. The focus is on God, not self or things.	Playtime Questions to Answer: Who has given us all things? Does God want us to enjoy the life, possessions, and things He has given us? How can we make a practice of remembering God when we are enjoying the things He has given?	God Gives Us Everything, Including Play We are happiest when we think about how God has made us happy. Thank God for Our Things Sometimes when we have a lot, we need to be reminded who gave it to us. God Enjoys Giving Us Enjoyment God's gifts are free expressions of His generosity.	God's Property Stamping desks, lockers, books, name-tags, even the school building with labels that declare "Joey's desk, on loan from God" would reinforce the theme.

94

Diagram #14 The Biblical Truth Working Your Plan

The Biblical Truth of Chores: Work Your Plan

Supernatural Revelation

Natural Revelation

Christian Life And World Studies

What must
I Know
Be
Do
because of
what I've
learned?

Passage (Biblical Foundation)	Principle (Scriptural Teaching)	Plan (Curriculum)	Point (Christian Understanding)	Project (Classroom Application)
"Be diligent to know the state of your flocks and attend to your herds..." Proverbs 27:23

"The plans of a diligent man lead to profit..." Proverbs 21:5

"Lazy hands make a man poor, but diligent hands bring wealth." Proverbs 10:4 | Plan Your Work & Work Your Plan The word "know" means to focus concentration upon something; "attend" means to direct one's mind to a task. Strategy, intensity, and commitment are necessary ingredients to finishing any chore. | Questions to Answer Why do we have to do this now? Can't we wait until later?

Activities to Include: Chores

Daily Assignments

Following a Schedule | Work is given to us by God: for our benefit and His glory. "Having something to do" is God's intention for enjoyment and productivity.

Chores are a Part of our Schedule People have to decide what they are going to do, put their mind to it, and do it. If God gives us something to take care of, we have to follow his orders in taking care of it. | Ahead in the Long Run Bring in special speakers that reinforce the idea. Long distance runners, doctors, carpenters, or business persons would be able to help children see that God's principle of forward thinking is positive and productive for all of life. |

95

Diagram #15 The Biblical Truth Repetition

The Biblical Truth of Chores: Day-In-Day-Out

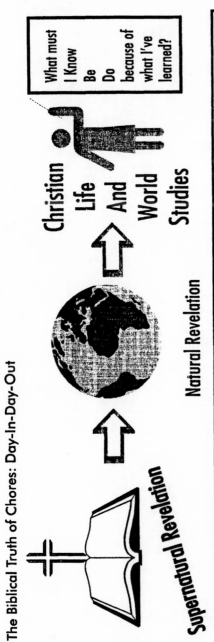

Supernatural Revelation

Natural Revelation

Christian
Life
And
World
Studies

What must
I Know
Be
Do
because of
what I've
learned?

Passage (Biblical Foundation)	Principle (Scriptural Teaching)	Plan (Curriculum)	Point (Christian Understanding)	Project (Classroom Application)
"Whoever keeps the fig tree will eat its fruit" Proverbs 27:18 "Do you see a man skilled in his work? He will serve before kings..." Proverbs 22:29 "The hard working farmer should be the first to receive a share of the crops" 2 Timothy 2:6	Regular, Repetitive, Routine, Rhythm of Life Daily patterns produce results. This kind of work is often referred to as "menial", "tedious", or "boring." But these words are a result of perspective and attitude. We should view nothing as "below me", small, or worthless. Rather, we should work hard now for tangible outcomes later.	Teacher's Helper Daily classroom chores Repetition in memory work	No 'Teacher's Pets' Here "He who looks after his master will be honored" (27:18) tells us that those who think the teacher "plays favorites" are really those who don't want to be "in the game." Showing You Care Day-in-day-out consistency, is rewarded by those who are in charge.	Create a Chart Have students develop a wall hanging reminder that keeps them responsible for routine tasks in the classroom. "Home" Work Partner with parents to identify duties that pupils can account for at their own house.

Diagram #16 The Biblical Truth of Maintenance

The Biblical Truth of Chores: Making it Last

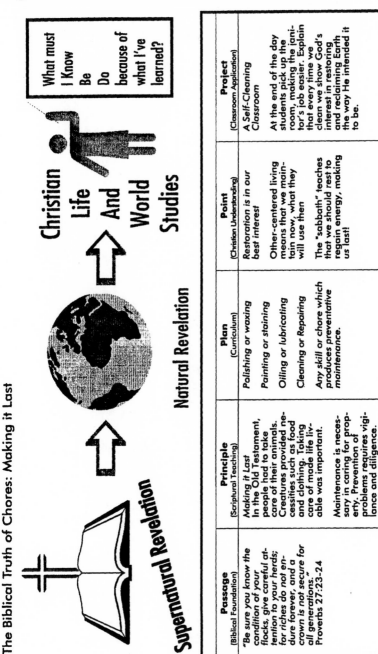

What must
I Know
Be
Do
because of
what I've
learned?

Supernatural Revelation

Natural Revelation

Christian
Life
And
World
Studies

Passage (Biblical Foundation)	Principle (Scriptural Teaching)	Plan (Curriculum)	Point (Christian Understanding)	Project (Classroom Application)
"Be sure you know the condition of your flocks, give careful attention to your herds; for riches do not endure forever, and a crown is not secure for all generations." Proverbs 27:23-24	*Making it Last* In the Old Testament, people had to take care of their animals. Creatures provided necessities such as food and clothing. Taking care of made life livable was important. Maintenance is necessary in caring for property. Prevention of problems requires vigilance and diligence. "Staying on top of things" is indispensable for the worker.	Polishing or waxing Painting or staining Oiling or lubricating Cleaning or Repairing Any skill or chore which produces preventative maintenance.	Restoration is in our best interest Other-centered living means that we maintain now, what they will use then The "sabbath" teaches that we should rest to regain energy, making us last!	A Self-Cleaning Classroom At the end of the day students pick up the room, making the janitor's job easier. Explain that every time we clean we show God's interest in restoring and reclaiming Earth the way He intended it to be.

Diagram #17 The Biblical Truth of Waste

The Biblical Truth of Chores: Use It Again, and Again

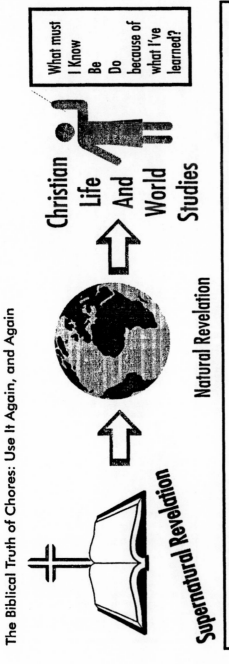

Supernatural Revelation

Natural Revelation

Christian Life And World Studies

What must
I Know
Be
Do
because of
what I've
learned?

Passage (Biblical Foundation)	Principle (Scriptural Teaching)	Plan (Curriculum)	Point (Christian Understanding)	Project (Classroom Application)
"When the hay...and grass is gathered in, the lambs will provide you with clothing, the goats with the price of a field. You will have plenty of goats' milk to feed you and your family and to nourish your servant girls." Proverbs 27:25-27	**Use It Again and Again** Cattle are fed, food is produced, work is accomplished for humans: taking care of something allows it to take care of you. The cycle of agricultural life in the Old Testament allowed people to prosper and pass on the proceeds to others.	Recycle, reuse, reduce Be careful not to waste	Renewable Assets Second Hand Shops Should be our First Stop "New" Does Not Automatically Mean "Better" Take Care of What You Have	The Next Generation Begin now to explain and illustrate how what we do now will affect people for years and years to come.

98

Diagram #18 The Biblical Truth of Labor

The Biblical Truth of Chores and Skills: Little by Little

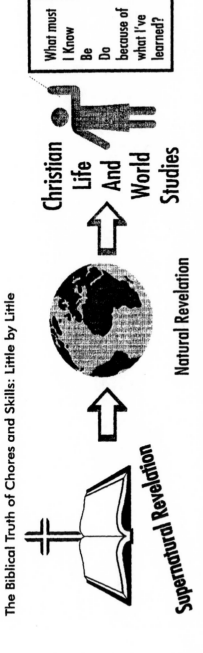

Supernatural Revelation

Natural Revelation

Christian Life And World Studies

What must
I Know
Be
Do
because of
what I've
learned?

Passage (Biblical Foundation)	Principle (Scriptural Teaching)	Plan (Curriculum)	Point (Christian Understanding)	Project (Classroom Application)
"You will have plenty of goats' milk to feed you and your family." Proverbs 27:25-27	**Little by Little** There were no long lasting "get rich quick" schemes in life. People worked hard for what they had. The farmer tended the fields, the fields fed the animals, the animals provided for the farmer. The gain was slow and steady. Profit does not normally happen all at once. Hard work brings "hard currency."	**Answering Questions** Why can't I have it now? Can't we do this quicker? Why do I have to do it?	Use What You Have Now Allow Assets to Work For You Gain is seen Incrementally Work Benefits the Worker	**Field Trip** Take your students to an old fort or settlement for reenactment of daily life chores. Have students participate in some way in projects that might reinforce the concept of hard work which produces something over time.
"...he who gathers money little by little makes it grow." Proverbs 13:11		**Asking Questions** What does working hard teach you about ...yourself? ...others? ...material things? ...patience?		
"All hard work brings a profit..." Proverbs 14:23				Discussion Investigate cultures where most of the day is spent in gathering and cooking food to eat. What would be the benefits and drawbacks?
"He who tills his land will have plenty of bread..." Proverbs 28:19				

99

Diagram #19 The Biblical Truth of Satisfaction

The Biblical Truth of Chores: A Worthwhile Job Well Done

Christian
Life
And
World
Studies

What must
I Know
Be
Do
because of
what I've
learned?

Supernatural Revelation

Natural Revelation

Passage (Biblical Foundation)	Principle (Scriptural Teaching)	Plan (Curriculum)	Point (Christian Understanding)	Project (Classroom Application)
"... the diligent man prizes his possessions." Proverbs 12:27	"Satisfaction" of a Worthwhile Job, Well Done	Any skill or chore which produces an increased, positive outcome for the person who works hard.	Investment	Taking Stock, Trading Stock
"Do you see a man skilled in his work? He will serve before kings ..." Proverbs 22:29	There is a sense of accomplishment for the person who works hard, sees the product of their labor, recognizing that all she has comes from God.		If you accomplish something it means more to you. You have put in time and effort. If something is given to you, it does not mean as much.	Set up your own "stock exchange." Have students work for a class project with a collective, cooperative effort which focuses on work, planning, and a projected outcome (e.g., lessened homework for beneficial production in class, time for creativity after accomplishing the times tables, etc.).
"When God gives any man wealth and possessions and enables him to enjoy them ... this is God's gift ..." Ecclesiastes 5:19	Pride focused on others is acceptable before God. He honors our labor because it is His		Getting Better, Getting More	
"... I take great pride in you..." 2 Corinthians 7:4			As a person's skill increases their ability to produce increases. This is God's law of production.	

Chapter 8
The Methods for Practicing Biblical Integration

"But how do *I* do it?" Knowing what something means, even modeling the concept does not always give the ability to practice the process. Day in—day out, lesson in—lesson out methodology will give the best opportunity for biblically integrative teaching. The method below is broken into four components with subsections. Notice that the first method is based on Bible study. That forms the basis for the other three: God's attributes, questions about life, and belief comparison.

Bible Study

As a person understands the Bible, he sees the transcendent principles and propositions that form the basis for Christian teaching. Following the model of biblical integration in Chapter 6, the examples below follow the application of truth that comes out of reading the text. The principle is stated in God's Word. The italicized comment is then linked to a concept taught in God's world. The teacher shows the whole or completed Christian truth as she interprets the world in the class. By answering the questions, "So what?", "Who cares?", and "Why should I study this today?," she helps the students see direct connections to real life. Making these kinds of statements in planned activities throughout the day demands the conscious commitment of the teacher to study the Bible and to practice Deuteronomy 6:7—repetitiously imparting application of God's law to life.

- Private property is assumed based on the eighth commandment (Exodus 20:18).

"Don't take something off another's desk; it doesn't belong to you."

- Animal rights are important as they were protected in Exodus 23:4-5.
  "Bird-feeders are good. Shooting robins with B-B guns is wrong."

- Hygiene is practiced because Leviticus 13 says not to spread disease.
  "When you go to the bathroom wash your hands."

- Research must be done since Proverbs 1:1-7 advocates increasing one's knowledge and wisdom.
  "Using the library helps to increase your understanding of a subject."

Leviticus 26:14-45 is an example of Bible study methodology that conveys the compounding consequences of sin over time. Principles from this passage could be applied in one or more of the following ways:

1. Establishing policy and procedure for correction.
2. Stressing the importance of maintaining a good reputation.
3. Answering the question of why repentance does not eliminate consequences.
4. Noticing why some people seem to get away without getting caught.
5. Learning from negative examples of behavior in others.
6. "Looking over one's shoulder" anticipating the worst.
7. Explaining why warnings are positive.
8. Recognizing the personal benefits of obedience.

Specific applications from this passage follow. Notice that questions are included in italics to help engage students in the learning process through dialogue. The biblical principles are drawn from what the text says and applied to school age children.

1. This is a warning for the future (v. 14, "but if..."). Rebellion against God has not yet happened. But if it does, it is because people ignored God's revelation (Matthew 11:20-24). People see what they should do and do the opposite (James 1:19-25). *Why are warnings good? Why do warnings sometimes irritate us?*

2. The reasons for sin's consequences (v. 14 "will not listen", "will not carry out"). God's people reject His laws or fail to carry them out (v. 15) because of stubborn pride (v. 19), hostility toward God (v. 21), or refusal of correction (v. 23). *Why do we say, "Why should I listen to you?" What are we communicating when we utter the phrase " I don't care what you say"?*

3. God uses other people to discipline (v. 16 "your enemies"). As a result of sin, those who may hate us prosper (v. 17). It's hard when those we can't stand benefit from our bad behavior. *How do you feel when your brother or sister—with whom you fight—gets privileges that have been taken from you because of discipline?*

4. Continued disregard for sin's consequences multiplies distress (vv. 18, 21, 23, 27, 28, "if after all this...if you remain hostile...if in spite of all these things"). Discounting additional warnings may increase the negative consequences. *Why is this true? What does a phrase like, "you're digging a deeper hole for yourself" mean?*

5. The normal flow of life will be interrupted (v. 16 "your life [will] waste away"). The usual will become unusual. The welcome will become unwelcome. The "boring" will become desirable. *Is the pleasure of the moment worth many moments of pain, discontent, and distress?*

6. Unconfessed sin causes us to wonder when the other shoe will drop (v. 17 "you will flee even when no one is pursuing" and vv. 36-37 "the sound of a windblown leaf will put them to flight"). *Do we enjoy anticipating the worst? The phone call to our parents? Being called to the office? Being discovered, found out?*

7. God takes an active role in the discipline of his children (v. 16 "I will punish"). We often forget that God hates, becomes angry and will judge (vv. 17, 18, 28). However, God never forgets His promise: "I will not completely abandon them or destroy them. That would put an end to the covenant with them and I am the Lord their God" (26:44). *What should be our view of God's discipline?*

8. The consequences of sin continue from one generation to another (vv. 39-40 "Because of their sins and their father's sins..."). We not only reap the effects of sin, but also may assume and extend the sin of our ancestors. *Can you give examples of how this looks in your life?*

9. People learn from the sin of others (vv. 40-41 "the sin of your ancestors"). *Why is it that we do not want to listen to the advice of others, especially of those who are older? Why do we say, "It'll be different for me?"*

10. Even after repentance the consequences of sin continue (vv. 40-43, "the full penalty for having rejected my laws and my commands"). Once the pendulum begins to swing it takes a while to stop. People may still "hold it against us". It may take years to regain a reputation lost. *How do we respond to people in authority when for some time after wrongdoing they seem to look for us to "blow it" again? Will we admit our wrongdoing or want to blame authority figures for discipline?*

11. The people of God, when disobedient, cause the wrath of God (v. 41 "which made me hostile toward

them..."). Judgment begins with God's people (1 Corinthians 11:31, 34; 1 Peter 4:17). *Why do we think sin is "out there" among others? Why are we so reticent to begin with ourselves?*

12. The penalty must be paid for sin (v. 41, 43, 44 "they will pay for their sin"). This has nothing to do with our salvation but with the consequences of sin. *Why is a penalty necessary?*

13. The obedience and disobedience of God's people seems to run in cycles (vv. 39-45 "generations"). When one generation disobeys and the next sees the process of sin and repentance, the next may see it and continue practicing righteousness. What ought to concern us is that our family follow our example. *Why is the role of godly parents, guardians, or mentors so important?*

Some scriptural statements are explicit; they can be taken at face value (e.g. Deut. 6:7). Underlying principles and implicit connections to individual truth statements also give authority about life. In a classroom setting, the teacher knows and reiterates the bullet-pointed Scriptural principles. These, then, interpret human life and its activities. For example:

- God gave humans responsibility to steward the world (Genesis 1:28; Ephesians 2:10).
  "Being the leader of your group is a big responsibility."
- God says economic opportunity and honesty applies to all people (Genesis 2:15; Exodus 22:1-15).
  "When you're playing games include everyone, be fair, and don't cheat."
- God initiated story telling to pass on truth (Genesis 1:3; Romans 15:4).
  "Reading books helps us to know how to live."
- God holds nations responsible for their actions (Genesis 11:1-9; Psalm 33:15-17).

"Sometimes countries we study in history make wrong choices."

Scriptural principles apply God's universal statements to all matters, all situations. "We take captive every thought to make it obedient to Christ" (2 Corinthians10:5). Thinking and teaching is for the purpose of restoring a Christian worldview. David acknowledged this by saying that all things belong to and come from God; what we give; He has given us (1 Chronicles 29:14-16). Any talents, possessions, or ideas we own, indeed, even our person comes from God. The soccer player, spelling bee champion, tuba player, entrepreneur, and artist must be reminded of this truth.

Psalm 67:2 makes another universal statement through the hopeful imperative "May your ways be known on earth." Heaven's conduct is possible to comprehend on earth. God's intension for human life is summarized in this brief avowal. God's "ways" might include ethical mandates, mathematical equations, scientific formulas, grammar rules, logic patterns, philosophical premises, political axioms, reading comprehension, athletic abilities, or dramatic flair. "Everything that was written in the past was written to teach us" (Romans 15:4). God's Word continues to establish principles of conduct for today. In the following citations, note the principles and possible applications:

Biblical Reference(s):
> *The earth is the Lord's and everything in it" (Psalm 24:1; 50:12; 89:11).*

Principle:
> Ownership of property must begin with God.

Applications:
> Nothing is "mine", nor does it "belong to me." Everything belongs to God. There are no "brute facts." The reason for giving or "tithing." God's ownership is the basis for economic theory, and individual property rights.

Biblical Reference(s):
> "Do you know the laws of heaven?" (Job 38:33).

Principle:
> Scientific law was designed by God and discovered by humans.

Applications:
God's laws of aerodynamics allow birds and planes to fly.
People breathe oxygen while plants breathe carbon dioxide.
Genetic materials can be traced and replaced. Astronomers
find *new* phenomena in space.

Biblical Reference(s):
"He establishes order in the heights of heaven" (Job 25:2).
Principle:
The interrelationship of all things finds it origin with God.
Applications:
Stars, rocks, and people all have different purposes but
have the same source. There are laws of interplanetary
movement. Rules of regulation for matter, motion, things,
and games are set in heaven.

Biblical Reference(s):
"The Lord looks down from heaven and sees all mankind...He
considers what they do" (Psalm 33:15-17).
Principle:
Nations and people are responsible before God.
Applications:
Good and bad kings rule. Treaties are broken and promises
kept. Secrecy and espionage; righteous and unrighteous;
military might and economic prosperity--everything is
monitored and registered under God's lordship.

Biblical Reference(s):
"God established all the boundaries of the earth" (Psalm
74:12-17).
Principle:
The physical world is regulated and restricted by God.
Applications:
The seashores, atmosphere, gravity, primary colors, time,
life, death, species, habitats, day, night, seasons, atomic
construction, gestation, reproduction, geography,
topography, were given set limits by God.

Biblical Reference(s):
> "God humbles Himself to behold…things on earth" (Psalm 113:5-8).

Principle:
> God stoops to humanity's level to show His care.

Applications:
> Rainfall, harvest, heat, cold, light, darkness, food, animals, vegetation, creativity, invention, ruler ship, service, are all invested goodness with human benefit in mind.

Biblical Reference(s):
> "Your hands made me and fashioned me (Psalm 119:73).

Principle:
> God participates in the formation of the human body.

Applications:
> Large motor skills, the interconnection between what is seen and unseen, muscles, bones, blood, cell structure, thought, emotion, and strength are intricate, discoverable, and wonderful all at once.

Biblical Reference(s):
> "Your laws endure to this day, for all things serve you" (Psalm 119:91).

Principle:
> Rules to govern all of life have their source in God.

Applications:
> The way the world, the human mind, government, science, literature, art, ethics, athletics, business, language, health, music, and administration was intended to work is a product of Heaven.

Biblical Reference(s):
> "He gave a decree that would never pass away" (Psalm 148:6).

Principle:
> God ordained all of human history

Applications:
> Nations, migrations, wars, peace, inter-generational ties, family trees, promotions, demotions, are found in God's eternal program.

Biblical Reference(s):
 "God formed the earth…to be inhabited" (Isaiah 45:18).
Principle:
 God made the earth for human occupancy
Applications:
 The earth exists not for the sake of the earth itself but for the glory of God and His vice-regent on earth, man. Occupancy privileges include caring stewardship and constructive invention.

Biblical Reference(s):
 "I brought Israel out of Egypt and the Philistines from Caphtor…" (Amos 9:7).
Principle:
 God is the Lord of nations and the Lord of history.
Applications:
 From the smallest events to the largest progressions of human history, God demonstrates His sovereign control of people, places and things. Nothing is insignificant and everything prominent.

Biblical Reference(s):
 "Surely the wrath of men brings you praise" (Psalm 76:10); "God does as He pleases with…the peoples of the earth" (Daniel 4:34-35); To Pilate Jesus said, "You would have no power over me if it were not given to you from above" (John 19:11).
Principle:
 Nations give God glory in everything that they do.
Applications:
 Political decisions, wars, and government leaders are ultimately controlled by God. Evil acts of men are turned to good by God. Nothing happens outside of God's providence.

Biblical Reference(s):
 "Every word a man speaks will be accounted at the judgment" (Matthew 12:36).
Principle:
 Nothing is hidden from God.

109

Applications:
> *Conversations are heard by God. Secrecy and privacy are impossible when we are responsible to an omnipresent and omniscient God.*

Biblical Reference(s):
> "God gives life to the dead...calls into being that which does not exist" (Ro 4:17).

Principle:
> <u>God raises the dead and creates from nothing.</u>

Applications:
> *From the womb to the tomb God orchestrates and organizes atomic particles and genetic codes. Cryogenics and in vitro fertilization, both the desire to extend and begin life are God's jurisdiction.*

Theological propositions deduced from inductive Bible study gives the basis for course instruction. The simplest statements are established by specific truth. The truth allows for application to life. Human statements reflect doctrinal belief.

- The Trinity (3 in 1) is the reason why there is unity in diversity.
  "The bottom number in a fraction is the whole; the top number in a fraction is part of that whole."
- Truth is the basis for practicing journalism
  "Always tell the truth."
- Humans made in God's image provide for proper race relations.
  "We respect all people, no matter their skin color."
- Human corruption is the reason for acts of crime.
  "Your friends didn't make you do wrong; you chose to do wrong."

In the following theological statements, note the principle and suggested classroom comments.

Theological Statement:
God is Invisible and an Invisible Spirit World Exists (Colossians 1:15-17).

Principle:
People should be careful not to limit knowledge to their senses or believe everything can be reduced to a natural explanation.

Classroom Comments:
"The results of the last election defy human understanding."
"Our eyes can deceive us. There might be more to life than meets the eye."

Theological Statement:
God Came to Earth as a Human: The Incarnation
(John 1:14-18)

Principle:
The care and concern we show for others is based on God's coming in flesh. Reaching down, He pulled us up to Himself. Reaching out, we give a helping hand to others.

Classroom Comments:
"Humanitarian aid to other countries shows the compassion of people."
"When we're nice to others we show them we care."

Theological Statement:
Salvation is by Grace Alone (Ephesians 2:5-8)

Principle:
Our standing with God is not dependant upon what we do but what He has done for us. We practice the doctrine of grace, the forgiveness of sin by God's gift of Jesus' sacrifice, by being gracious to others.

Classroom Comments:
"Don't worry about paying the money back; the loan is excused."
"You hit me yesterday but I'm not going to hit you back today."

Theological Statement:
Peace Made Through Christ's Sacrifice(Ephesians 2:14-18)
Principle:
Since humans broke God's law, payment is due. But Jesus took our judgment upon Himself. As Christians, we are no longer at war with God. Heaven declares us righteous by Jesus' death on the cross.
Classroom Comments:
"Let's see if we can bring the two parties together through arbitration."
"Don't be concerned about the past; it's water under the bridge."
"I'm not mad anymore since you said you were sorry."

Theological Statement:
Taking Communion: A Celebration of Christ's Sacrifice (1 Corinthians 11:17-34)
Principle:
We remember Jesus' body and blood given for our sin by using bread and wine as symbols. This is a physical action that reminds us constantly of a spiritual truth.
Classroom Comments:
"We have a day off from school today to remind us of a great past event."
"When we go to church we remember that we are part of Jesus' family."

Theological Statement:
God is Just (Deuteronomy 32:4)
Principle:
Standard for accountability is God's righteous character. Any calculation or evaluation in daily life mirrors God's fairness.
Classroom Comments:
"Math answers are absolutely right or wrong because God is just."
"Sometimes wrong things happen and we have to make it right."

God's Attributes

The characteristics of the Creator set standards for understanding life. We should uphold God's justice in the study of history. Medical ethics should be premised upon the worth of the individual as made in God's image. The person of The Almighty sustains mathematical concepts. We reflect God's nature in our nature.

- Accurate calculation in math is possible because God is Just.
  "Using a ruler or a calculator is how we get exact measurements."
- Ethical standards exist because God is Eternal.
  "Don't change the rules in the middle of the game."
- Art is produced because God is Creator.
  "Painting and drawing are good ways to express ourselves."
- Reading is possible because God spoke.
  "Learning to read and write helps us communicate with others."

How is the nature of God reflected in creation and His creatures?

- Holiness: God's set-apartness is our distinctiveness.
- Omniscience: we know as God gives us knowledge.
- Immanence: As God shows care for us, we show concern for others.
- Incomprehensibility: as God is beyond our understanding, so His creation mystifies and perplexes people.
- Revelation: God has communicated truth to us, we communicate truth of Him, to others.

- Existence: Reality is seen and unseen. God's invisible nature is displayed in visible *nature*. God's existence is the basis for ours.
- Personal: God has a plan for, communion with, and resides within His people.
- Eternal: Time tells us that we are temporal, limited, and yet have hope.
- Creator: As creatures we creatively create from creation.
- Aseity: God's self-sufficiency is mirrored in our independence as people, while we are dependant upon our Creator.

How do creation and His creatures respond to the nature, character, and attributes of God?

- Omniscience: As bearers of knowledge, we use logic, rhetoric, wisdom. *The ways we learn are based on patterns ordained by God.*
- Immanence: As God cares for creation, we practice health and counseling. *Caring for people shows the interest of God through us.*
- Holiness: As God is set-apart, we think Christianly, differently. *Christians begin with distinct foundations of thought.*
- Incomprehensibility: As God cannot be understood fully, we use philosophy, theology, and problem solving in an attempt to solve difficult problems. *Supernatural mystery and tension in life tells us we don't know it all.*
- Revelation: Because God has spoken; we speak, listen, reflect, and meditate. *We process God's thoughts and communicate His truths.*
- Existence: Since God is yet cannot be seen, we study geometry, physics, and space. *What we do on earth was initiated in Heaven.*
- Personal: Since we are persons replicating God's personableness, we investigate

psychology and sociology. *Relationships bear the marks of God's providence*

- Eternal: Since God plans based on a future, we strategize forthcoming events. *Commitment to afterlife, affects decisions in this life.*
- Creator: Imitating God's creativity, we accomplish enterprise and entrepreneurialism. *Artistic ventures in any field reflect God's design.*
- Aseity: We mirror God's self-sufficiency by research, reading, and thought. *Analysis is an attempt to complete <u>what</u> we don't know and recognize as humans <u>how much</u> we don't know.*

'Going on a diet' is the wrong use of the word 'diet'. Following the concept of God as creator, dietary intake should be a regimen focused on gaining daily needs as established in Genesis 1:29.[1] Similarly, exercise does not debilitate but rejuvenates. Exertion should be seen not as an act of depletion but of creation. Pain, a result of sin, is also a gift of protection from God. Flashes of information telling us not to touch the hot stove, saves our human tissue from destruction. Health, as designed by The Lord, has preventative medicinal value. Wellness for people is the intention of The Creator. Complaints about "boredom" in any age group could be countered by important questions. "Does a world of the 'normal', 'usual', or 'mundane' give us stability? Why or why not?" "If we lived in a world of chance, do you think we could expect less order and more disease, disaster, and calamity? Why or why not?" "How does the truth of a regulated creation give us answers to these questions?"

Questions About Life

Thinking God's thoughts after Him and formulating questions at times moves us toward answers. Human, worldview, and philosophy queries[2] lead educators and students alike toward truth. A Christian response using six interrogatives everyone asks can help to begin the process of thinking Christianly about every theme and subject. Human questions might look like this:

115

1. *Who* is responsible for sustaining the world?
2. *What* lessons do we learn from gym class that come from God's Word?
3. *When* do we "worship"?
4. *Where* do wrong choices begin in humans?
5. *Why* should we protect human beings from disease, abuse, or death?
6. *How* can we use our money so that we honor God?

Some people think in terms of "themes" or "subjects". Scripture speaks to many topics addressed throughout life and literature, prompting ideas for biblical integration. The most important question is "Why?" Why we study a discipline is based on belief. Why suggests a reason for doing something: if there is a purpose, there must be some kind of hope for the future.[3] "Why do we have to spell correctly?" or "Why is learning vocabulary important?" are questions teachers might hear.

Motivation—or why we do the things we do—is important for everything. Human incentives could include: realizing that the Lord knows human motivation (Proverbs 16:2), knowing that giving is for others' benefit rather than our own (Matthew 6:1-2), being more anxious for human praise over that of God's (John 12:43), remembering that reasons for our actions will someday be exposed (1 Corinthians 4:5), or knowing that the reason why things don't work out the way we may want is because of self interest (James 4:3).

Victory and defeat are constant refrains in life. Sometimes we learn more from failure than success. Jesus' example of apparent defeat and ultimate triumph suggests that our view of winning and losing is different than that of God's (cf. Colossians 2:15). Gain and loss are spoken of often in The Bible (cf. Matthew 10:39; 16:25). Principles derived from their application might include the gain of greed is ruin (Proverbs 1:19), whereas wisdom trumps money as a commodity to be had (Proverbs 3:14). Ripping people off will ultimately benefit others (Proverb 28:8), whereas the righteous person, who rejects extortion, is the one who is individually blessed by God (Isaiah 33:15-16).

Others-in-relation-to-self is a key scriptural concept. The Trinity sets the standard for *sharing the spotlight* by these precepts. The Spirit glorifies the Son (John 14:26; 16:13) and The Son glorifies The Father (John 8:54). Doing unto others (Mark 12:30, 31) is often spoken, and little practiced. Better to put into practice Jesus' self-deprecating approach to life (Philippians 2:1-11). In Scripture there are no commands to love oneself, rather to love God by loving everyone else (Mark 12:30, 31; cf. Ephesians 5:28, 29). Similarly the Trinity is the intended pattern for human community based on the fellowship in the Godhead prior to creation (John 17:4, 25).

Time and its uses are a grave concern for humanity. This life is not a dress rehearsal. Children should learn early that time cannot be *saved* nor should it be *wasted* or *killed* (Psalm 39:4-7). The present should be spent remembering the past (Psalm 77:10-12) while anticipating the future (Psalm 71:14-18). Ephesians 5:16 literally means we are to *buy up every opportunity*. Planning requires a suitable exercise of allotted time. Since man "does not know his time" (Ecclesiastes 9:12) it is proper to prepare for death (cf. Luke 12:15-21), accounting for how each moment is spent (Psalm 90:7-12). Every tick of the clock should remind us that we will die and we are responsible to use our time wisely.

Other themes which Scripture addresses include: authority, boredom, diet, energy, freedom, money, pain, priorities, problems, relationships, sex, and worship. Common questions might be addressed with biblical answers: "Can I have it all?" "What happens when people disagree?" "Do I have to...?" "Why can't I?" "Can we go outside today?" "How much longer?" Since Scripture clearly gives parameters for thematic understanding, the Christian schoolteacher is responsible to help students see the biblical view of all things.

Book themes address common human and biblical concerns. *Horton Hears a Who* stresses the individual worth of all people. The benefits of money are subjective and change according to the story *Alexander Who Used to Be Rich*. The power of confession and forgiveness is the basis for *The Scarlet Letter*. Attempts to usurp God's moral order end in horror in *Frankenstein*. An evolutionary treatise portrayed as a 'dog-eat-dog' world is the view of Jack London in *The Call of the Wild*.

William Golding, in *The Lord of the Flies,* wrote that humans left to themselves will always degenerate. Sovereign intervention in the life of a slave is the backdrop to *Amos Fortune: Free Man.* The *Bridge to Terebithia* is an important catharsis for death counseling. Status does not equal worth in *The Prince and the Pauper.* The answer to what is real can be found in *The Velveteen Rabbit.* Problems with power and human nature no matter who the leader may be are the main themes in *Animal Farm.*

The Big Questions

Worldview questions[4] connect abstract belief to life on the street. Everyone asks questions upon which they base their beliefs: (1) What's Real? Are there things we can't see? (2) What's Known? How do I know anything? (3) What's Best? Is there right and wrong? (4) What's Man? Who am I? Why am I here? (5) What's Next? What happens when I die?

What's Real?

Is there a supernatural world and why might it matter? Following the migration of the Puritans from Europe to the New World demonstrates the hand of God moving people. *We're Going on a Bear Hunt* explains that getting to where we want to go means, "we have to go through it".[5] This primary story reinforces the idea of life, as it really is, not as what we want it to be. Christian teachers must organize their instruction around the world the way God intended it to be. Children can still play 'make believe' but imaginary friends and places are rooted in a young one's experience of what already is. Reality cannot be re-imagined.

Who is God?

Could Jesus' two natures in one person give an indication of why light can be described as both a particle and a wave? God's person has reflected in His world many ways; perhaps this is one. Math functions can be checked against each other because a standard of truth exists. Children learn that standing on a chair adds to their height when reaching for candy on the shelf. In a similar fashion they learn that a picture may need to be cut subtracting from its size to fit in the frame.

Math works because God is the unifying presence in the world. *Who* is the source and harmonizer of all things (1 Corinthians 8:4-6). Photosynthesis and reproduction stress the same point. The abilities for growth and replication pre-exist within the genetic code of plants. God made the world to be self-sustaining and self-regulating (Genesis 1:12, 29-31). The periodic table reflects patterned order. Original work by Dmitri Mendelev, a Russian chemist, who discovered facts about physical elements and the British scientist Henry Moseley, who discovered the atomic numbers of the elements 50 years later, show God's world to be sequential. Element properties align the rows and columns of the periodic table into patterns that cannot be rearranged as they have a basis of course outside themselves. Kenneth Grahame's *The Wind in the Willows* points toward God when Rat and Mole encounter *the holy place* in chapter seven. Met by the August Presence, Rat responds to Mole's question of fear, "Afraid?" murmured the Rat, his eyes shining with unutterable love, "Afraid! Of *Him*? O, never, never! And yet—and yet—O, Mole, I am afraid!" What better portrait of The Almighty's transcendence and immanence combined![6]

What's Known?

How can I know if the author is right? How can I believe the latest news report? Can we know it all? Among others, these questions begin students down the road of Christian inquiry. Interpreting literature from a Christian context has been greatly helped by the publication of various texts including *Invitation to the Classics*[7]. Along with background information about ancient through modern authors, the volume elucidates worldview issues with a series of questions for the classroom specifically designed for believers.

Ferreting out the truth in reporting is the role of a journalist. Allowing everyone to tell his or her side of the story in his or her own words is crucial, producing reporting which is fair and balanced. C. John Sommerville in *How The News Makes Us Dumb*[8] suggests that the world learns more from wisdom and history than a constant barrage of information. Surely Paul's words reverberate the same message throughout the pages of Scripture, "ever learning but never coming to a knowledge of the truth" (2 Timothy 3:7). Doing research of any kind, organized Christianly, recognizes that knowledge comes from God (Proverbs 2:1-8), is passed through a grid of evaluation (2:9), changes a person's perspective (2:10), and provides future assessment tools (2:11). Field-testing and experiment replication follows the biblical imperative that "in the multitude of counselors there is safety" (Proverbs 11:14; 15:22; 24:6).

What's Best?

A biblical view of ethics runs counter to cultural mores from any period. People, left to themselves, will choose standards that are: (1) Personal: How does this affect me? (2) Relative: Isn't everything in a state of change? (3) Experiential: Isn't my conduct governed by what feels good? (4) Popular: Doesn't the majority vote rule? and (5) Situational: How can doing what is right now affect actions later when circumstances change? Christian ethics rest upon transcendent, immutable, objective, and universal tenets. Law comes from outside human beings, never changes, and is impartial, affecting everyone, everywhere, at all times.

What's a Person?

Primary children need to learn early that the bad things people do are a result of what they think in their mind. Taking responsibility, accepting blame, practicing confession, and receiving forgiveness follows a pattern set down in The Bible (Psalms 32 and 51). High schoolers should be made to confront the current beliefs of society about human nature. Questions about human behavior being the product of psychoses, genetics, or surroundings must be countered with clear Christian teaching on inherent corruption (Mark 7:21-23; Romans 3:9-20). On the other hand, why people do good things is an outcome of a conscience created by God (Romans 2:14, 15). Motivations may corrupt why good is accomplished (cf. Matthew 6:5). The Holy Spirit could motivate the spirit of a person, moving them to practice virtue (cf. John 16:8). Or God may have specifically designed a person's life to do His bidding (cf. Isaiah 44:28-45:1). Whatever the case, being good at heart is due to God's spirit rather than our own. Whether the discussions are concerned about how I am different from my dog, musical lyrics from popular culture, or the roots of racism, questions about humanity are clearly addressed in The Bible.

What's Next?
Knowing that "bad guys" will get theirs is dependant upon future justice (cf. Psalm 73). Expectations of any variety draw on a commitment to anticipation (cf. Matthew 11:1-6). Birthdays and celebrations are remembrances that honor the past while anticipating the future. God set up the generational pattern (cf. Genesis 5, 10) where family history, memories, stages of life, and accomplishments could be commemorated (Leviticus 23-25; Psalms 105 and 106). *I will* in Scripture is always based upon *I did*. The past is the launching pad for the future. God's promise to care for His people was often tied directly to the historical event of The Exodus from Egypt (cf. 2 Samuel 7:23). The fact that Jesus came to earth the first time is why He will come again (cf. Acts 1:10, 11).

What people do now they do because they desire or want something else. This is eschatology: the study of future things. Why anyone does anything—planting a tree, learning an alphabet, practicing a free throw, playing music, solving a mathematical problem—is directly linked to the fact we believe in the future.

Other Questions
Intention, corruption, and reconciliation questions[9] show that the pattern for human behavior was established in Genesis 1-11. (1) Generation: What was God's intention for _____ (whatever I teach) in Genesis 1 and 2? (2) Degeneration: What affect did sin's corruption have on _____ (whatever I teach)?, (3) Regeneration: What reconciliation of _____ (whatever I teach) can occur when completed through biblical principles?

For example, work is for human benefit, producing from and protecting creation (Genesis 1:28; 2:15). A teacher might stress to students that they do *their jobs well so that they will take good care of what's been given to them.* This follows God's established pattern. Exodus 20:7 orders that God's name not be misused, which would make it meaningless.[10] Addressing a class who needs a reminder of a proper response to God, a statement such as *"Being profane or irreverent belittles God and makes light of serious issues"* could make the point. "Love songs" should emphasize sacrifice and unconditional love according to The Song of Solomon. Current products available to young people should be countered by declarations stating the obvious, *"Music videos don't show respect for women: they honor sex as love."*

Sometimes it is only a small distortion of truth that changes the perception of things. Something good becomes bad. Light, created by God, became the center of worship in the sun god Ra in ancient Egypt. Shinto, the religion of *the rising sun,* explains that Japanese emperors were descendents of the sun. The fall disjointed humanities' view of light causing the creation to be placed in the role of the Creator (Romans 1:18-25). Yet, there are redemptive usages of light. Medicinal therapies ranging from diagnostic tools such as the MRI to the benefits of vitamin D from sunlight can be used regeneratively for good. Light is upheld in Scripture as a created thing under the jurisdiction of Heaven (cf. Isaiah 60:19-20). Likened to agents of light, Christians continue to reflect "the light of the world" (Philippians 2:15).

Through Drama

Drama or understanding the stages of life should be approached Christianly. Director's notes based on their study of the script, background, and playwright should interact with the themes presented in the performance. Pre-play monologues teaching an audience what to expect from the play, giving hints as to it's proper understanding, would be an apt introduction to every performance. Post-play discussions with the audience engendering interaction with the people in the seats about the story's significance for the Christian worldview would be a grand conclusion to each production. Rehearsals that instruct the actors about the point of the story and how to communicate it Christianly are a necessity. Considering what theme, worldview perspective or human question a play may answer is worthwhile. Thinking how the director's notes, practices, and actors might incorporate the Christian identification of error or unification of truth in the production is crucial. An example of generation, degeneration, and regeneration takes place after the curtain rises, recreating pieces of God's story in three acts:

Act I: Creation
  1) The Creation is God's (Psalm 24:1: 50:12; 89:11).
  2) What We are, God has Given (1 Chronicles 29:14, 15).
  3) The Creation Reveals God to Us (Psalm 19; Romans 1).
  4) We Express our Joy in Creation through our Creative Gifts (Ecclesiastes 5:18-20).

Drama gives humans the opportunity to magnify God, not us. Drama, therefore, is not an end in and of itself. Drama expresses something above and beyond this life. Drama is an act of worship, showing delight in God-given talent, enjoyment of life, and God Himself.

Act II: Corruption
  1) Sin distorts God's Creation (Genesis 3; Romans 8:18-22).
  2) God Continues to Display His Glory in Creation (Genesis 5:1-3).
  3) Conflict between Righteousness and Rebellion Plays out through Creatures (Genesis 4; 1 John 3:10-12).
  4) We Cannot be Righteous Apart from God (Genesis 2:16, 17; 15:6; Romans 3:27, 28; 5:1, 2).

Drama displays both truth and falsehood. Drama mirrors The Creator through the creature. Drama follows, displays, and comments on the battle between right and wrong, good and evil. Drama teaches that humans have a need for redemption that cannot be self-obtained.

Acts III: Correction
  1) God redeemed corrupt creation at the Cross (Ephesians 1:20-23; Colossians 1:13-20).
  2) Humans know there is a need for redemption (Ecclesiastes 3:11; Acts 16:27-34; Romans 1:18-19).
  3) God initiates and completes redemption in a human life (Ephesians 2:1-10; Titus 2:11-14)
  4) God uses Christians to speak the message of redemption (2 Corinthians 5:17-21).

Drama allows humans to recreate situations and characters that display the need for God's redemption. Drama shows that humans know something is missing, that people seek redemption. Drama can explore human questions and divine solutions to redemption. Drama is an opportunity for believers to point toward correction of creation's corruption.

The play *Pygmalion*[11] provides a vehicle for demonstrating the process of thinking Christianly. George Bernard Shaw, the author of *Pygmalion*, was no friend of The Church. Throughout his writings, Shaw allows his disdain for God's Bride to shine through. Shaw was a Marxist-Socialist and accepted Nietzsche's "superman" image of humans. In his desire to achieve a "higher life", however, Shaw claimed Bunyan's *Pilgrim's Progress* among his favorite books. His desire to abolish poverty and inequality were based upon his belief that people had to be good. As a socialist he believed science could change a person for the better. *Pygmalion*'s central tenet, then, is that human involvement is the only tool needed to change a person.

Shaw leveled his broadsides against his own English culture. He believed that the English had no respect for their language and would not teach their children to speak it. The satirical nature of *Pygmalion* also revolts against the English class system. That the lower classes were mistreated is clear in Shaw's play. Shaw says that while people can be transformed by laboratory skill, what matters most is that they are still people.

While the believer cannot accept some of Shaw's basic assumptions about life, there are still pieces of truth to be found. For instance, the biblical understanding of discrimination points out that the intrinsic nature of an individual matters more than outward characteristics or circumstances. *Pygmalion* clearly makes this point. However, though Shaw did not like prejudice he had no basis within his own worldview to hold such a perspective. Shaw's just cause is borrowed from the Bible.

Tennessee Williams' play *The Glass Menagerie* is considered by many to be autobiographical. Guilt, loss, and anger create the undertow of the drama. Hope seems to be just out of reach. Phrases like "if I had only..." or "if I had to do it over again..." can be read between the lines. Escape is an unfulfilling option: people may leave a place, but the place is still in the people. After a long run we discover our problems are tied, string to ankle, rattling and clanging after us. As one character says, "What are we going to do? What will become of us? What is the future?...I'm just bewildered by life."

The Christian can look at this play recognizing a number of counterpoints within Christianity. The Christian lives life as he finds it, recognizing earthly inequities, difficulties, and sadness (Psalms 39, 49, 73, 88). Yet biblical hope is not a possibility premised on "perhaps." Christian hope is sure, certain, personal. As the hymn writer penned, "All our hopes and fears are met in thee tonight." Future assurance is based on the One who made it possible.

Juror #8 takes a stand by making his colleagues in the jury box take a stand for *their* beliefs. Set in the 1950's *Twelve Angry Men,* originally performed on television, was rewritten for the stage. A minority seems to have been the perpetrator of murder causing most of the bigoted adjudicators to assume his guilt from circumstantial evidence. It seems that social pressure and racial discrimination may have swayed those who are determining guilt or innocence.

This play demonstrates two components that are essential for justice to be done: logic that trumps emotion and law that is essential to the character and applicable to all. It could also be stated that law, being the central theme of the play, is the only advantage for the disadvantaged. Christians, more than anyone else, should be most interested in fairness because there is no justice if it's left up to just us. We know that Jurisprudence is premised upon unchanging, heavenly truth (Ecclesiastes 3:16, 17).

Belief Comparison

Students from upper elementary through high school would especially profit from this method of biblical integration. It encourages them to evaluate error with the truth they know—a skill that imperative for Christians (cf. Hebrews 5:11-14; 1 John 4:1[12]). Truth exists and must be acknowledged in other viewpoints as remnants of God's intention. Error must be "sorted out" to demonstrate the insufficiency of variant worldviews. Christians

125

ask, "What problems are there with the philosophy, framework, and reasoning of anything?" A Christian should always say, "If I take this too far, I could end up over here. What biblical principles would help me to avoid the pitfall?" Consider the following examples.

- Reincarnation teaches there is an afterlife, which is true. But falsehood also exists in its teaching. This eastern philosophy also teaches that there is a repetition of lives, that judgment is played out through successive lives, that justice is based on good works outweighing bad, and that sin is not personal or serious (cf. Ecclesiastes 12:13, 14; Hebrews 9:27).

- Self-esteem stresses human dignity, a concept dependent upon being created in God's image with which Christians agree. However, denying self and practicing humility are the commands for believers (cf. Mark 8:34; 1 Peter 5:5, 6).

- Achievement is accomplished through hard work, not feeling good about one's self. Awards are not given simply for showing up, rather for contributions that add to understanding or that benefit the group. Curbing wrong behavior (fighting, drug use, or slander) is not dependent upon a child self esteem but upon admitting one's sinfulness and turning from rebellion against authority (cf. Titus 3:1-11).

- Computer technology gives speed and access to a wide variety of information that helps people—surely a biblical incentive. But community is lost with the impersonal nature of cyber-tools. Dependence upon information and knowledge alone leads to positivism and humanism. Stress on computer labs and classes in education place priorities on technique above wisdom and discernment in understanding elemental truths of history, ethics, the afterlife, and human purpose. Computers should be seen as tools—beneficial when utilized properly, detrimental to those reliant upon them (cf. Ecclesiastes 1:12-18).

- Compare Greek and biblical concepts of heroism. Upon review one discovers that a Grecian view was man-centered, while biblical views of heroism recognized the source of human strength and accomplishment in God (cf. 2 Corinthians 3:5; 4:7).

- Compare the 'gods' of other cultures to the True God. Similarity does not equal sameness. While Greek mythology attributes certain attributes to the gods, the fact that they are created, changeable, or uncaring in comparison to The Personal Eternal Creator emphasizes how much more important differences are over similarities (cf. Isaiah 44:6-8).[13]

- Compare the movie "Dead Poets Society" with a Christian concept of education. The film is propped upon two insidious lies: old thinking is wrong and free-thinking is possible. Christians should recognize that every thought is based on or developed from the thought of another. The ability to think is corrupted by sin, which contradicts the possibility of pure, autonomous thought (cf. Matthew 15:19).

- Compare the authorial intent in Arthur Miller's play *The Crucible* with a historical view of Puritans and the "McCarthy era" as a whole. Are all sides seen objectively? Are labels used properly to examine what people believe? How is Miller's worldview communicated through his writing? (cf. Deuteronomy 19:15-18; Proverbs 18:17).

Through Decision-making

A Christian understanding of how to make decisions could be based on the Pauline model in Romans 15:15-24. The apostle identified his philosophy (verses 15-18), purpose (verses 20-21), plans (verses 15-19), priorities (verses 23-24), even citing his perseverance (verse 22) in accomplishing the goal. Believers and unbelievers alike apply transcendent truth when they evaluate a situation, make choices, recognize consequences, and apply resident wisdom around them from trusted sources.

Untruth in decision making often stresses individualism—doing what's best for you, legalism—doing what human authorities tell you is best for you, and relativism—doing what you determine is best for you. A Christian corrective stresses: the limitations of knowledge—human and selfish (Proverbs 11:19;

14:12; 16:25); that knowledge comes from an outside source—it is trustworthy (Proverbs 8:22-31); that knowledge is defined by wisdom (Proverbs 1:1-7); that repositories of wisdom on earth include historic examples (2 Kings 23:24-25); and present counsel (Proverbs 19:20; 20:18), and future possibilities (Titus 2:11-14; hope gives a reason for making right choices)

Through Textbooks

Addressing the model or theory proposed in a textbook is one approach to practicing belief comparison. An anatomy book may say that speech organs (i.e., the tongue, lips, or teeth) are biologically adapted for phonate use. It may say vocalization is primarily a survival tool.[14] The Bible, however, teaches that Creator—creature communication was the intended purpose of speech. This is not only an important philosophical component in a Christian school biology class, but in a speech class, as well.

Consider how a music textbook may reason that music is for purely aesthetic pleasure or based solely on the taste of the individual. A Christian approach to music recognizes the beauty of God's glory, which is music, and art's true focus. *Art for art's sake*, where the interpretation is up to the viewer, is a prominent perception in some aesthetic circles. A Christian school music instructor should help students to redeem the true premise of art, namely, a reflective creation on the world as it is mirroring the Artist of all creation.

A mathematics textbook may state that mathematics is neutral, created by humans, and that it is totally pure and used only for practical purposes. Yet Christians know that mathematics is God's language whereby He created His world. Mathematics was created, is discovered, can be abused, and has a theological underpinning that allows it to function in God's world.

Through Literature

In a Christian school English class, book reports should interact with the author's view of life evidenced through the theme of the book and compare and contrasted these themes with a Christian perspective. Louisa May Alcott's semi-autobiographical *Little Women*, for example, was a reflection of her own Christian home life and ideals. Mark Twain's view toward The Church, on the other hand, was anger-laden and his view of life descended deeper into depression and a dark abyss of rebellion toward God as he grew older. *Where the Wild Things Are*, a children's story, suggests that disciplining one's passions and training one's imagination is paramount, surely a Christian theme. An ancient tale, "The Sword of Damocles," correctly moralizes the problem of power. *Pinocchio* was a bad little boy who needed redemption in the original story written by Carlo Collodi, whereas Disney's version teaches the perversion that the puppet was good at heart. Shakespeare's *Macbeth* teaches properly that man is culpable for his actions, yet also teaches that he can exonerate himself by facing his doom courageously—a philosophy full of humanistic hopelessness. No one thinks, reads, writes, teaches, or lives in a vacuum. An author's worldview will always display itself on the pages of his book.

In journalism classrooms teachers must teach the objective quality of truth and the need for primary source material in belief comparison. Assignments, interviews, photo opportunities—everything right down to the captions—must challenge the journalist's integrity. Journalist ought to consider the following questions:

1. Am I being fair and honest in my reporting of the facts?
2. In what way might someone think that I'm trying to 'spin' the news?
3. Is there a conflict of interest in my reporting?
4. Do I have a personal axe to grind?
5. Am I listening to all sides, acquiring multiple considerations, concerns, and interests?
6. Do I ignore certain news stories or points of view, selecting only those who voice what I want heard?
7. Does ridicule, minimalization, or marginalization of different perspectives shape my stories?
8. Is word choice an important component in writing script?"

National Public Radio runs a program called *All Things Considered*. Listeners of this broadcast might ask themselves the above questions while critiquing such a show. A Christian approach acknowledges the views of multiple witnesses

(Deuteronomy 19:15-18), and proposes to listen to both sides of a story before prior to judgment (Proverbs 18:17). The power of words is obvious and carries with it great journalistic responsibility (Proverbs 24:12, 24-26; 25:15; 26:23-28; 29:19).

Through Governments

Comparing beliefs includes evaluating worldviews in ancient documents—a practice that would certainly be necessary in a history class. For instance, *Hammurabi's Law Code* mandates death for stealing. *The Pentateuch* (the first five books of The Bible) requires death for premeditated murder. The first law elevates property over people; the second highlights God's view that we should love people and use things, not the other way around. The *Ennuma Elish*—a Babylonian myth of earth's creation—describes fickle, finite, self-centered gods who create human beings for the express purpose of lessening their own workload. People are seen as useable resources rather than protected individuals, made in God's image, whose intended role on earth is to co-reign with The Sovereign of the universe, as in the biblical account. The Hippocratic Oath was enacted to protect humans from scurrilous physicians. "To do no harm," is the first consideration when someone needs medical assistance. Medical, ethical boundaries mirror the Christian concept that people should be protected.

Public policy should also come under the scrutiny of belief comparison, a practice that would be useful in a political science class. For instance, transcendence must form the foundation for our belief about individuality, groups, rights, and privacy. In courtrooms this is called *natural law*: a decree outside ourselves. *Autonomy* (self-law) is antithetic to a biblical worldview. While we celebrate diversity, creativity, and individuality, we must recognize that all we are and all we have is from God (1 Chronicles 29:14).

Communitarians say that a group can decide what is right and wrong, resting their arguments not on any person but upon society at large. Theirs is only an error of larger proportions compared to the autonomists. Who says what the needs of a group are? What is the standard for *the common good*? If the state *gives* rights, isn't anyone afraid they might also take them away? The famous statement from Proverbs 29:18 "where there is no vision, the people perish" gives us direction. The Hebrew word for *vision* means revelation or law. There must be a set of tenets that establishes community law—apart from the community. "All authorities are instituted by God" (Romans 13:1; 1 Peter 2:12). The government *does* bear responsibility to mete out justice. Yet, central government can be corrupt (Proverbs 29:2, 4, 7, 12, 14, 16) and only The Judge can be fair (29:26). Ecclesiastes clearly teaches that justice is impossible if it's left up to just us (3:16-4:3).

Privacy itself is really impossible from a Christian viewpoint. God's omnipresence and omniscience mitigates any *aloneness*. Not only will everyone's works be judged in the next life (Ecclesiastes 11:9), no one can run from God in this one (Psalm 139:1-7). However, privacy among humans is still a reality. Three universal principles concerning privacy follow:

1. A homosexual bookstore contained two bumper stickers in a glass display case. One read, "Keep the government out of my bedroom". Next to this was another: "The government has blood on its hands: support AIDS research". Some desire to live a *carte blanche*—blank check—sexual lifestyle without bearing individual responsibility for the results, expecting others to take responsibility for their actions. The famous statement, "you can't have your cake and eat it too," still applies. The first universal privacy principle is this: "If you break it, you've bought it". Accept the blame without excuse. God is the final judge, in any case (Hebrews 4:12, 13).

2. The second amendment to the United States Constitution guarantees the right to keep and bear arms. If elected officials proceed to restrict private ownership of firearms through licensing and registration, confiscation of firearms may well result. The second universal principle of privacy is to punish the criminal and not restrict the liberties of law-abiding people. Enough laws exist to control crime. Government must enforce *these*. Constraining the rights of all by not punishing the few is wrong (Exodus 22:28-32).

3. Materialism is a noxious concept to the Christian mind. But property rights are sacrosanct (Exodus 20:15,17). Personal property provides people with a means to live. Creativity and freedom within a market economy explodes into prosperity. The third universal principle of privacy is clear: if God is The Creator of all, we are responsible to honor Him by honoring each other's property since it all belongs to God anyway (Leviticus 25:23; Deuteronomy 6:10-12; 8:10-20; Psalm 24:1). Privacy should be understood as God-given and individual-driven.

For further explanation of belief comparison, examine the examples in Activity #8. Notice that the biblically integrative principle forms is the foundation for what is being taught in the curriculum. The principle could well have multiple applications in various curricula. Communication to the students shows how the concept might be taught Christianly. Using the biblically integrative principles below, practice how a Christian teacher might use them in his or her classroom.

ACTIVITY #8: SHOWING HOW IT WORKS IN THE CLASSROOM

Biblical Principle	Curriculum	Communication
God communicates with language (Psalm 33:4-11)	Grammar: What is the difference between a noun and a verb?	Careful communication with each other is important because God communicates with us.
God designs patterns in creation (Psalm 148:1-6).	Math: Group by tens	We can organize and count because God organized His world.
All people groups are important to God (Genesis 12:3; Revelation 5:9, 10)	History: Immigrants coming to America	We should welcome all races and ethnic groups because all people are the same to God.
The functions of God's world were set at creation (Jeremiah 33:2, 20-21; 25-26).	Science: The properties of magnetism.	Scientific laws can be observed because God governs His world with working, natural authorities.
Why should we protect human beings from disease, abuse, or death? (Ex 21:28-32).[15]		
What happens when I die? (Heb 9:27).[16]		
Technology gives speed; but community is lost because it is impersonal (Acts 2:42-47).[17]		

Chapter 9
The Means Through Which
Biblical Integration is Practiced

If "the earth is The Lord's, and everything in it" (Psalm 24:1; 50:12; 89:11) then our teaching must include His universal understanding. Biblical principles cross disciplines and lead to the demonstration of Christ's lordship in all things. For example, the teaching of demonology in 2 Peter and Jude saturates C.S. Lewis' *The Screwtape Letters* in literature class. Cross-cultural understanding of spiritual warfare in missions, perceiving the human response to truth in counseling, discipleship in student development or the supernatural battle of human suffering in psychology are all woven with interrelated principality and power truths discovered in these and other epistles. In a similar way, interdepartmental biblical integration could link Scriptural principles among the intelligent design movement in science, cosmology in apologetics, intentional health planning in lifetime fitness, a critique of "Inherit The Wind" in drama, comparison of creation mythology in history, and "God's handiwork" hymnology in music.

One of the most famous Scriptural principles is what many refer to as *the cultural mandate* from Genesis 1:28 and 29: "God's intention for humanity was to manage and conserve, not use and abuse, the creation. Both production from and preservation of earth's resources are possible".[1] In the examples below, ranging from primary through high school grades, note how the principle of caring for and creating from the natural world crosses curricula and intersects with other biblical thought. For practice, Activity #9, after reading each integrative principle, write an idea of how that Biblical concept might be used in the classroom or curricula.

Four Approaches to Biblical Integration

Teaching spans all age groups and all subject areas. Are there ways to understand books, events, ideas, people, and places so as to be more inclusive? By developing strategies to appreciate (1) books, (2) subjects, (3) the humanities, and (4) the mathematical fields from a Christian perspective a teacher might begin the process of constructing their own grids for the Christian school classroom.

Consider how the biblical concepts from the preceding or following pages might permeate instruction in any of the instructional approaches below. Be aware of how *principled permeation* unifies truths, identifies errors, and codifies instruction. Note the following examples for each approach.

Approach #1: Through Books

Author, Book, or Theme: How did the author approach their work? Did the author's background influence their writing? If so, how? Can the answers to the five worldview questions be seen in the writings? Can the Christian teacher agree or disagree with the perspective developed in the book? What error should be exposed? What truth originating in God's Word should be acknowledged?

Approach #2: Through Subjects

Subject, Unit, Lesson or Concept: What foundational principles or ideas does the subject assume? What Christian explanation or clarification of the discipline must be realized? What further Christian concepts need to be addressed throughout the succeeding lessons? Is the textbook correct in its assessment of the facts, beliefs, interpretation, or selection of information?

Approach #3: Through Humanities (History, Arts, Psychology, Sociology)

Worldview: What is the basic assumption being made? Proponent: What did the major contributor believe? Policies: What rules did governments document based on the work produced in the fields of history, the arts, or the "soft sciences"?

Consequences: What was the end result of the belief system established?

Approach #4: Through Mathematics (Sciences, Biology, Chemistry, Physics)
Idea: What was the hypothesis? Research: What did the surveys or statistics suggest? Experimentation: What did the findings show? Result: What would happen if the theory was acted upon or followed through to its completion?

Specific Examples Using These Four Approaches

Approach #1: Through Books
The Sign of the Beaver, by Elizabeth George Speare (New York: Yearling Books, 1984, reprint, softcover). Speare loved researching history and bringing the people of other times to young readers.

Biblical Integration Principles
- <u>Humanness transcends culture.</u> Attean and Matt were first and foremost people. Tradition or lifestyle differences don't matter as much as accepting others for who they are. Everyone is made in God's image (Genesis 1:26) coming from His "family" (Ephesians 3:14).
- <u>We can always learn something new about the world from another's point of view.</u> Attean and Matt each offered something of value to the other. We should be anxious to learn, slow to speak, humbly acknowledging that someone might know more than us. Christians should watch for ways to help not hurt others (Proverbs 3:27-31) and be eager to be taught (Proverbs 12:15; 13:10).

Biblical Integration Questions
1. Can humans of different cultures live together in prosperity (see page 87). Apply Scriptural statements such as Romans 12:18.
2. Should people attempt to change another person's culture or the way that they live? Why or why not? What is the difference between customs and ethics in a civilization?

3. Is compromise possible when there is such a stark contrast between people groups and the way they live (see pages 65-66)? Explain.
4. Was it right for Euro-Americans to come to *the new world*? Was it right for settlers to take the land? See pages 116-117. How does Psalm 24:1 and Leviticus 25:23 relate to this issue?
5. What do the similar flood stories suggest on page 70? Could it be that common truth comes from a common source? (see Acts 17:24-28 and Ephesians 3:14). Should we learn from others and be happy for new experiences? Explain.
6. Why are *Robinson Crusoe* and *The Bible* such important books in the story? What does this tell you about the author or the period of time in which the story takes place?
7. The Native Americans didn't believe the Euro-Americans should only kill animals for their fur. Matt had difficulty accepting that Attean spoke to animals as if they were the same as humans. Is either way right? Why or why not? What would the Bible say about both points of view?
8. Matt discovered why Attean didn't have a good attitude toward European settlers later in their relationship. What does this tell us about relationships with people we don't know? [For instance, we sometimes jump to conclusions or make assumptions; we should be considerate of peoples' past.]
9. Can only Native Americans write about their culture? Can people tell stories about cultures other than their own? Why or why not? How should we tell stories about others from a Christian perspective?

Approach #2: Through Subjects

Hygiene. In God's providence, the passage of time has allowed humans to advance technologically so that methods and means of daily living have changed. While "breakthroughs" and "new frontiers" have emerged, the basic principles of God-given life in creation have remained constant. Consistency in the creation order has allowed advances in discovery while maintaining universal truths in all arenas of life. Scriptural texts reflect the substance of these verities. It is the responsibility of the Christian educator to bring these standards "forward" to the 21st century.

For Example: Health codes and personal hygiene are premised upon sanitation regulations written in Scripture. Passages such as Exodus 29:14, Leviticus 12:1-4, and Deuteronomy 23:12-14 provide universal principles that reside within these contexts:

1. Contagion: Concern over communicable diseases necessitated the quarantine of sick people for the community's protection.
2. Sanitation: Concern for cleanliness was both personal (i.e., preventative medicine) and corporate (i.e., zoning to maintain distance between people and waste).

In Interpretation: Health and hygiene are God's interests when delivering the quarantine edicts of Leviticus 11-15. Because infectious bacteria and viruses can live for up to 48 hours in an open environment, God's law forbade people with communicable diseases from reentering the social setting for *seven days*, effectively eliminating the threat of contagion for others.

In Application: Everyday concerns for everything from washing hands to hair nets in food preparation, garbage dumps to sewage systems in community planning, prevention to restoration in the medical field provides the ethical basis for hygiene.

Historical Connections:
- Discuss the living conditions of the European communities that succumbed to the bubonic plague.
- Discover how Jewish settlements during the 14th century were different. Note application of OT law.

Pedagogical Connections:
- Watch clips from the film *Outbreak* to demonstrate the care with which researchers treat disease.

- Research the history of disease control to see how it has improved throughout history. Team-teach with the science teacher using labs about disease and hygiene.
- Read Philip Yancey and Henry Brandt's books *Fearfully and Wonderfully Made, In His Image,* and *Pain: The Gift No One Wants* for further truths found in the natural world whose origin is from the supernatural realm. An older work containing marvelous insights from Scripture about biology is *None of These Diseases* by S.I. McMillen.

Approach #3: Through Humanities

Psychology. *Future of An Illusion* by Sigmund Freud stated that God as *father figure* was self-generated. Freud based his theory on two assumptions: (1) Humans make up God for emotional help and (2) God doesn't exist outside of one's own mind. Along with the teaching of social Darwinism that the strong survive and the weak die, Freud's viewpoint helped to formulate the doctrine behind the totalitarian dictatorships of the 20th century. The end result was a term coined by the atrocities committed against whole people groups: genocide.

A Christian Response:

1. The Problems with Freud's Research
- His Samples were based on interviews of the mentally ill
- Other psychologists have shown Freud's analysis to be fraudulent
- Great, human intellectuals have been theists and Christians
- History is neglected. There is documentary evidence of Jesus. His claims to Godhood can be reasonably argued.

2. The Answers to Freud's Assumptions
- "Humans create a 'God' for emotional help.
  ...If theists are emotionally troubled, why have believers created so many social agencies to help people? Disturbed people do not focus on others.
  ...Psychology cannot disprove God's existence since as a 'science' it can only comment on observations about people.

...Believing in God changes peoples' lives. A person's outlook on life may be benefited by a radical transformation acknowledging God as source and sustainer.

- "God doesn't exist outside the mind of a person"
  ...Everyone begins with assumptions. In this case, either God is eternal or matter is eternal. Freud had 'faith' that God did not exist. Just because Freud taught this presupposition does not make it automatically true.
  ...If God exists as the Personal Eternal Creator, how can finite creatures make the infinite Creator? If the supernatural does exist it is obvious that natural explanations would be insufficient.
  ...Just because I can't experience something with my five physical senses does not eliminate the possibility of that thing's existence. People believe in 'love' yet cannot scientifically demonstrate the passion in a test tube. [Notice Festus' response to Paul's defense of Christianity in Acts 26:24-29. Times may change, but human nature does not.]

Approach #4: Through Mathematics

Statistical Analysis. Mathematical precision is essential to launch a space shuttle. Probabilities and outcomes may be properly predicted by *crunching numbers*. However, examination of figures for various research projects in *hard* or *soft* sciences must be recognized for what they are: variable and interpretive. Any number of inconsistencies can skew the result of findings. Every hypothesis brings with it certain beliefs. Surveys, statistics, and polls might suggest a course of action or a general belief but should not qualify as a final solution. Experimentation must have unambiguous controls. Of course, the question of "Can we do it?" and "Should we do it?" demarcates values versus ethics. If quantitative analysis forms the sole basis for public policy, the assumptions of a few may undermine the free flow of information for many.

As with the study of any discipline, selection and interpretation of data will always be the baseline of analysis. Someone will decide what is said and how the information is conveyed. Human nature will in some way distort results. Because people enjoy *story* more than *hard facts* they will be drawn to the emotional elements of a movie like *John Q* while being unaware or ignoring the limitations of life in the situation the film portrays.

Some Problems with Statistics
1. Scientific Studies may include one or more of the following problems: omissions, semantics, presuppositions, political agendas, cultural acceptance, traditional beliefs, moral *neutrality*, personal experience, poor logic, misinterpretation, and poorly designed experiments[2].
2. Polling data must be evaluated in light of the following: reputation of pollsters, methods to obtain random data, the size of the sample, wording of the questions, rate of response versus non-response, sponsorship of poll, and interpretation within context of other data[3].

Solutions in Using Statistics

1. Peer review
2. Educating journalism about research
3. Comparative Analysis
4. Multiple sources of information
5. Distinguish between editorial and credential comments (someone who reports versus someone who knows)

Unit and Lesson Plan Biblical Integration Samples

Training the next generation of Christian schoolteachers to think and teach Christianly at Moody Bible Institute has produced some wonderful examples of real-world instruction. Notice that the unit plans are the foundation of each subject. Principles identified are then brought to bear on the discipline at hand. The ideas are universal in scope so that language principles relate to all dialects and history tenets relate to all cultures. Consider the following unit and lesson plans.

Unit Plan Integrative Ideas

Lesson One: Language was God's Idea and Gift to Us
- Humans have language because they are made in God's image (Gen 1:26)
- God the Father, the Son, and the Holy Spirit communicated with each other before God created mankind (Gen 1:26; cf. John 17:5, 24)
- As we listen and speak, we reflect a God who listens to us and shows Himself to us (Lev 10:3; Jer 9:24; Ps 5:3; 2 Chron 7:14; John 14:21)
- As we are creative with language, we reflect God's creativity (Gen 1:5, 8, 10; 2:19, 20)
- Language forms relationships. Before the Fall, communication was open and honest (Gen 2:25). Sin distorted communication (Gen 3:1-6). Selfishness caused people to be deceitful, attempting to control God and others with their communication (Gen 3:9-14).

Lesson Two: The Beginnings of Different Languages
- God designed language to establish unity (Gen 12:1-3). In order to work together as team, people must be able to communicate.
- After the Fall, humans chose to use their unity to rebel against God rather than to be unified under God's authority (Gen 11:1-4).
- God intervened and confused the languages so that the people could not work together against God and so that people would return to God's plan for them to fill the earth and subdue it (Gen 11:5-8).
- God wants His children to be attentive and responsive listeners (Ex 14:14; Deut 6:4; 2 Kings 17:14; Neh 9:29; Is 30:15; 1 Tim 2:2; James 1:22-27).

Lesson Three: Language and Loving My Neighbor
- God commands us to love our neighbor as our self (Lev 19:18)

142

- Loving the stranger is part of loving our neighbors (Lev 19:34; Deut 10:19)
- Jesus emphasized loving strangers (Matt 25:31-46; Luke 10:30-37)
- Loving our neighbor brings joy (Prov 11:25). Fulfillment is a by-product of self-sacrifice (Gal 5:22)
- Ignoring the command to love your neighbor is incompatible with loving God (Matt 25:31-46, 1 John 4:19-20)

Lesson Four: Reaching Out in Friendly Greeting
- The value of the individual is based on being valued by God (Matthew 10:26)
- We must value others (especially strangers and outcasts) because God values them as His image-bearers and people for whom Christ died (Rom 14:15)
- We must reflect God's love to us by loving others (Col 3:12-15; 1 John 4:19)

Lesson Five: Getting to Know Others through Introductions
- Our sinful tendency is to be self-absorbed (Phil 2:20-21)
- God takes interest in us (Gen 16:13; Ps 139:1-4). We ought to take interest in others (Phil 2:4)
- The Bible commands that we identify and empathize with others (Rom 12:15)
- Love is not self-seeking (1 Cor 13:15; Phil 2:5-8). The motivation for our friendships should not be personal gain, but God's love (2 Cor 5:14)

Lesson Plan One Integrative Ideas

Objective One: Students should be able to demonstrate an understanding that communication was God's idea, expressing in their own words that the members of The Trinity communicated before we were even created.

Play a recorded tape of Genesis 1:26-27 read by a deep bass voice. Ask "Who is the 'us' God is referring to?" (The Trinity) "Who was the first person to have a conversation?" (God, The Trinity) Have students read

143

Leviticus 10:3; Jeremiah 9:24; 2 Chronicles 7:14; John 14:21 asking them to listen for words like "listen," "speak," "hear," or "show." Emphasize that these words are all communication words. God listens to us and reveals Himself to us. Whenever we listen and speak, we mirror God's communication.

Objective Two: Students should be able to recognize language as a gift from God, responding in thankfulness to Him.

Students bring their favorite stuffed animals to class. Read Genesis 1:5, 8, 10. Ask, "Who decided that day would be called 'day' and night would be 'night'? (God) Read Genesis 2:19. Ask, "Who decided that a hippopotamus would be called 'hippopotamus'?" (Adam) Using animal crackers, dividing the class into small groups have students invent funny, new names for the animals. Ask, "Do you think Adam had fun naming all the animals? Do you think it was hard? Why are we able to create new names and come up with new ideas?" (Because God gave language and creativity.) Teach the song "If I Were a Butterfly" in Spanish stressing through prayer and praise thanks to God for language to know Him and His creation.

Objective Three: Students should be able to explain how language was distorted by sin through a specific example.

Watch the video "The Rumor Weed". Discuss with the class the danger of lying and spreading rumors. Ask, "Have humans always used language in such negative ways—to hurt, control, or tear down people. Ask students to recall what they learned in objectives one and two. Ask, "What made language 'bad'?" (sin) Ask students for examples of language distorted by sin. Have students color large pre-made tagboard letters that spell out these questions, "Is it true? Is it kind? Is it necessary?" Explain each as the students color.

Social Studies, 7th Grade, Understanding the History and Culture of China[5]

Unit Plan Integrative Ideas

Lesson One: The Chinese, God's People

- All humans were originally made in God's image but due to the Fall, have become shattered image bearers (Genesis 1-3)
- All humans were created to bring glory to God. However, with separation between God and man, self-glorification was produced (Psalm 2, 90, 104)
- It is important to understand the different cultures around us. (Acts 17:16-24)
- It is important to evaluate our perception of cultures, identifying personal biases (Leviticus 18:1-5)

Lesson Two: The History of the Chinese

- Generation: God personally directs the affairs of man— nothing happens outside of God's design and all things happen for God's glory, including the rise, and the fall of nations. God's in control of the smallest detail to the grandest event. Even though the events of the past are sometimes a mystery, all events are sovereignly interrelated (Isaiah 44-46; Daniel 1-6; Romans 8-9; Ephesians 1).
- Degeneration: Man attempts to manipulate or reshape history in order to fit his own agenda (cf. 1 Samuel 15). Man is also blinded by his own self-centeredness and is unable to see God working behind the scenes in history. Man often thinks he controls his own destiny. (cf. Pharoah's refusal to acknowledge God in Exodus 4-14).
- Regeneration: History must be seen through God's eyes in order to get the proper perspective of different events (cf. the history of the small nation of Israel in human affairs). God's people must have faith to know that God is working for His own good and His glory because most of the time we cannot see the underlying purposes (Romans 8:28; 2 Corinthians 5:7).

Lesson Three: The Communism of China
- Because government officials are leaders with God-given authority, they should protect the freedom of the individual with the fewest restrictions applied (Deuteronomy 17:14-20; 1 Samuel 8:10-18).
- Mankind cannot live autonomously because of his depraved condition (Genesis 1-11; Psalm 2, 14, 39).
- Equal opportunity is not the same thing as equal outcome. The distribution of resources fails to account for a fallen world with inevitable and personal irresponsibility (Deuteronomy 32:4; Psalm 98:14; Leviticus 19:36; Deuteronomy 16:18).

Lesson Four: China Today
- Generation: God created human relationships with others to reflect the relationship of The Trinity (Genesis 2:21-25; John 17:20-23).
- Degeneration: This unity was destroyed in the fall (Genesis 3:1-6). Sin in humans produced blame (Genesis 3:9-13), barriers (Genesis 3:14-16), and burdens (3:17-19). Human attempts of reconciliation are inadequate and cannot be done in human strength alone (Genesis 3:7-8).
- Regeneration: Relationships with others can only be completely reconciled through salvation through Jesus (Galatians 3:26-28). This is the only solution to the problem because God is the only one who can satisfy the requirements (Genesis 3:21) and ultimately eradicate sin (cf. Genesis 3:15).

Lesson Five: China and You
- Followers of Christ are in the world, but should not be of the world (John 17: 1 John 2:15-17).
- Through the Bible it has been commanded of God's people that they share their faith with the pagans around them (Deuteronomy 4:6-8; Matthew 28:19).

Lesson Plan Three Integrative Ideas

Objective one: The students should be able to define communism and demonstrate its strengths and weaknesses in comparison to the Christian worldview.

> *In cooperation with other 7th grade teachers, whenever an assignment is assessed a grade of "C" will be given no matter how many right or wrong answers are on the paper. When the students question or complain the response will be "I'm the teacher. I can do what I want." The next period students will assemble ideas in a guided note taking setting regarding the tenets of communism. In journal form, they will reflect on their thinking concerning the previous day's experience of grading. A discussion will follow answering questions about control of resources and equality of outcome and opportunity. Students will organize the pros and cons of communist government on the board adding the ideas to their notes and comparing these to biblical viewpoints.*

Objective two: The students should be able to identify the significance of the Cultural Revolution and how it characterizes the depravity of man.

> *A brief outline will be given in class about the Cultural Revolution in China. Read the chapter "The Propaganda Wall" from <u>Red Scarf Girl</u>, which portrays the struggle of loyalty between Mao Zedong and the awareness of evil in his policies. Students will write a response paper to the question, "From what you know of the Cultural Revolution, how do the events that took place exemplify man's depraved nature?"*

Objective three: The student should be able to criticize the philosophy of communism using Scripture.

> *Divided into "Communists" and "Christians" the class will debate their positions using their textbook and class notes.*

Science, 3rd Grade, The Solar System[6]

Unit Plan Integrative Ideas

- Genesis 1:14-20, The creation account of God creating the sun, moon, stars, and seasons shows us God's consistent patterns.
- Psalm 19:1-2, "The heavens declare the glory of God" will be the memory verse for the entire unit.
- Jeremiah 31:35, The Lord Almighty is the ruler of heaven and His heavenly creation declares His power.
- Psalm 113:1-6, As long as the sun rises and sets, the name of the Lord is to be praised (cf. Isaiah 45:5-6).
- Psalm 148:1-6, Praise God for His faithfulness as seen through His creation of the heavenly bodies.
- Psalm 136:1-9, Give thanks to the Lord because His love endures forever and His creation speaks of this great love and power. He is the great Creator worthy of all praise and worship.
- Deuteronomy 4:19. When we look up into the sky and see God's handiwork, it should draw us to worship and praise His name. We should always worship the Creator, not the creation.

Lesson Plan Integrative Ideas

Objective: The student should be able to explain the temperature of the sun, the reason for shadows, the effect of the sun on humans and other parts of creation, and the various purposes of the sun.

Outside, the students will spend five minutes listing as many things as they can find that are located in sunlight and shadow. Place a lump of clay on the sidewalk to see what will happen to it over time. Place a stick in the ground next to a sidewalk marking the shadow of the stick throughout the day with chalk. Discuss how the earth rotates around the sun. Use a magnifying glass to show the power of the sun's concentrated light on a piece of wood. Discuss with the children what Scripture states concerning

the sun (using the biblical integration ideas above).
Discuss the activities of the day understanding how they
happened based on the previous discussion.

Math, 10th grade, Tessellations[7]

Unit Plan Integrative Ideas

- The order of the creation reflects the order of The Creator (Genesis 1).
- God's delight in symmetry and beauty is evidenced in His creation (Jeremiah 31:35-37).
- Tessellations depict God's eternality since a tessellation can go on forever (Exodus 3:14 ; Psalm 90:2).
- God is the Designer-Creator. Tessellations exhibit the patterns that He put in place (Isaiah 46:10, 11; John 1:1-3; Colossians 1:16).

Lesson Plan Integrative Ideas

Objective: The student should be able to value the construction strength of tessellations in tiles and walls.
Review shapes including the concept of polygons. Have the class note tiles on the ceiling and floor. Encourage examples of other tiling polygons inside or outside the classroom (including brick buildings or sidewalks). Discuss the design and strength of a honeycomb. Compare and contrast creation constructions with human blueprints. Construct patterns of predictability based on the discussion. Have the class develop a simple philosophy of math statement based on biblical truths evidenced in creation.

Math, 6th grade, Probability[8]

Unit Plan Integrative Ideas

- God is finite, humans are finite (Genesis 1; Job 38-42; Romans 11:33-36).
- Omniscience, knowing all, describes God's character about information (Psalm 19:12-14; Isaiah 40:12-14; 1 Timothy 6:10-12).
- God is sovereign: there is no such thing as chance, luck, or accidents (Isaiah 46:9-11; Ephesians 1:9-11).
- Ethics are based upon a transcendent (outside), immutable (unchanging) source of truth. "Fairness" must be based on these concepts while it is understood that perfect equality is impossible in a sinful world (Isaiah 59:1-15; Romans 2:1-11; 2 Thessalonians 1:5-10).
- Since God is separate from His creation He is outside of probability (Genesis 1).

Integrative Lesson Plan Ideas

Objective: The student will be able to participate in and evaluate fairness through playing a game called "Special Sums".

Each player in a group of three rolls two number cubes five times adding their rolls recording scores based on a certain number of points (if 1-4, player A gets a point, if 5-8, player B gets a point, if 9-12, player C gets a point). Discuss the following questions after the game: Did you like the game, why or why not? Is life like the game, why or why not? Is life fair, why or why not? Are our actions evaluated by rules that we like, why or why not? What benefits or disadvantages do my actions afford me or others? How do our actions reflect our view of God? Can life ever be fair if I don't "control the roll of the number cubes?"

150

Literature, 12th grade, The Picture of Dorian Gray, by Oscar Wilde[9]

Unit Plan Integrative Ideas

- Christians must evaluate the ideas of people through the lens of Scripture (Proverbs 3:21-26; Matthew 10:16; Romans 16:17-19; 1 Thessalonians 5:19-22; Hebrews 5:11-14; 1 John 4:1-6)
- The biblical basis for beauty is internal rather than external (1 Samuel 16:7; Proverbs 11:22; 31:10; Isaiah 3:16-26; Matthew 23:37; 1 Timothy 2:9; 1 Peter 3:3-4).
- Fulfillment and pleasure come to people who acknowledge that God gives life as a gift to be enjoyed (Ecclesiastes 2:24-26; 3:11-15; 5:18-20, etc.).
- Pride is self-promotion based on the assumption that man can be autonomous (Genesis 3; Proverbs 6:1-5; 11:2; 12:15; 14:16; 15:32-33; 16:18; 18:12; 1 Timothy 3:6; James 5:16).
- Humanity is inherently corrupt, yet sin is still a choice (Genesis 3; Psalm 51:5; Romans 1:18-32; 3:1-14; 5:12; Ephesians 4:18-19; Titus 1:15; James 1:14-15).

Lesson Plan Integrative Ideas

Objective: The student will be able to explain Wilde's contention that everyone sees their own sin in Dorian Gray.

Using an overhead statement of Wilde's purpose statement "Each man sees his own sin in Dorian Gray" discuss how we can relate to Dorian Gray. Discuss the attraction of sin through the characters of Basil Hallward and Sybil Vane. Have students write a poem expressing the darkness of their own hearts. Choose a video clip highlighting this theme. Do an interdisciplinary study with psychology pointing out the biblical truths that permeate the study of human behavior with the literary themes found in Dorian Gray.

Core Course Philosophies in Biblical Integration[10]

Each discipline in a Christian school should be premised upon a biblical foundation. Christian theology must permeate the philosophy and objectives of each scope and sequence.[11] With the help of Christian educator Douglas Osborn, I have documented below four foundational principles for each of the four primary disciplines: mathematics, science, literature, and history. These principles and additional support materials are available in poster format through www.biblicalintegration.com.

MATHEMATICS

1. Arithmetic answers are right or wrong because God is truth.

Biblical Basis: 1 Kings 17:24; Psalm 31:5; 119:160; John 14:6; 17:17.

"God [is] the pillar and foundation of truth" (1 Timothy 3:15)

Biblically Integrative Mathematics—Any truth in God's cosmos immediately precedes from God's character. From this premise, corollary principles follow for math: Math is (1) transcendent, originating outside human reason; (2) absolute, unaltered to fit surroundings; (3) verifiable, standing up to checks and correction; (4) exclusive, correcting answers assumes falsehood; (5) universal, whose operations exist everywhere, all the time; (6) sensible, working because it is true; (7) practical, conforming to the created world; and (8) consistent, always the same as before.

2. Math shows how the whole and the parts fit together because of the Trinity

Biblical Basis: 1 Corinthians 8:4-6; Ephesians 1:3-14; Colossians 1:17

"in Him all things hold together" (Colossians 1:17).

Biblically Integrative Mathematics—During the Middle Ages the word "university" was used to identify the place where students studied how "the one and the many" fit together. Only the Trinitarian Christian worldview has the answer. "Three persons in one essence" suggests that God created the cosmos to mirror His nature. In the world there are distinctive "parts" given meaning through the unified "whole". Math proves that the universe has a cohesive unity. Mathematicians must compare their equations to what already exists. Answers to problems must be compared to how the world works in reality. Math is not a human invention but a discovery of one of God's creation languages. God is The Personal, Eternal, Creator. Since He is *personal,* math has significance. Because He is *eternal,* human understanding of math is limited. Being the *creator,* God shares His ability to create math with humans.

3. Mathematical patterns are predictable and reliable because a faithful, dependable God established them.

Biblical Basis: Genesis 8:21-22; Deuteronomy 7:9; Jeremiah 31:35-37; Malachi 3:6; 1 Corinthians 1:9; Hebrews 13:8; James 1:17.

"God appoints and decrees the sun, the moon, the stars" (Jeremiah 31:35-37)

Biblically Integrative Mathematics—God compares His promises, dictates, and laws for humans against the standard of those regulations set for creation ("appoints", "decrees"). In fact, God states that the mysteries of the universe reflect the mystery of His nature (Job 11:7-9). A stable universe is necessary for the world to operate properly. Math does not "work" unless God's order is established in creation. Order makes logic possible. Logic sets patterns. Patterns allow people to build. Building assumes predictability. Prediction is only possible if there is stability; something one can count on.

4. The precision, accuracy, and exactitude of measurement are rooted in God's justice, shown through His perfection.

Biblical Basis: Deuteronomy 32:3-4; Isaiah 59:1-15; Matthew 5:48; Romans 2:1-11; 3:19-20.

"His works are perfect, and all His ways are just." (Deuteronomy 32:4)

Biblically Integrative Mathematics— God's nature is mirrored in 'nature'. A study of mathematics reveals the structure and order of the physical world and gives students insight into mind and character of God its Creator. Through mathematic discovery, humans begin to understand the precision of God. Properly understood, mathematics is the language God used to make His universe. Mathematical concepts must be linked to God's created world to make them meaningful to the student. This can be accomplished by practical application of mathematical concepts. Many modern approaches to teaching mathematics often isolate mathematical concepts from real world experience and teach mathematics for the sake of mathematics alone. By using God's knowledge revealed in math, humans give God glory.

SCIENCE

1. God is the sovereign Lord, Creator and Sustainer of all.

Biblical Basis: Genesis 1; Psalm 33; Romans 1; Colossians 1:15-17

"For by Him all things were created: things in heaven and on earth, visible and invisible, whether thrones or powers or rulers or authorities; all things were created by Him and for Him. He is before all things and in Him all things hold together." Colossians 1:16-17

Biblically Integrative Science—The creation is a focus on the Creator not the creature. God does what pleases Himself, for His own purpose and glory (Isaiah 43:7; 46:9-11; Psalm 135:5-7;

Ephesians 1:9-11). All questions concerning life (i.e., God, humanity, purpose, reality, knowledge) find their answers in the supernatural (Deuteronomy 30:11-20). Remembering Who maintains life's source is a key to human choice between righteousness or rebellion (Genesis 4, 11; Deuteronomy 28). If all life is God's, human response should be to (1) worship The Creator with the best of one's livelihood (Genesis 4:4); (2) undertake the role of tenet with God as landlord (Leviticus 25:23); and (3) give excess of production benefiting everyone with all the gifts bestowed by God (Deuteronomy 26:10-12).

2. God gave man responsibility to rule over the animals, and to develop and protect the earth.

Biblical Basis: Genesis 1:26-30; 2:15-20; 9:1-4

"God blessed them and said to them, 'Be fruitful and increase in number; fill the earth and subdue it. Rule over the fish of the sea and the birds of the air and over every living creature that moves on the ground.'" Genesis 1:28
"The Lord God took the man and put him in the Garden of Eden to work it and take care of it." Genesis 2:15

Biblically Integrative Science—"Earth Day" is every day. Care for creation is given from The Caretaker: it's His world (Psalm 50:10-12). Since sin corrupts everything, the good that people do or produce can harm the world and people (i.e., relentless acquisition of property for personal gain at the expense of the poor, cf. Amos 8:4-6). But the definition of "rule" in Genesis 1:28 suggests management and conservation. God's laws protect both man and beast (cf. Exodus 23:4-12). Business and "environmental" groups can cooperate. God's written word is to bring us back into right relationship with Himself which is accomplished through right relations with creation (cf. Leviticus 25:1-7; 2 Chronicles 36:21). Future earth dwellers will do that for which Eden was intended—fruits of labor create wealth, health, joy, and benefit for all (Isaiah 60-61).

155

3. God established consistent laws to govern all aspects of His creation.

Biblical Basis: Jeremiah 31:35-37; 32:2, 20-26; Psalm 33; 119:91; 148:6; Nehemiah 9:6.

"For he spoke, and it (the world) came to be, he commanded, and it stood firm." Psalm 33:9

Planes can fly, buildings stand, and machines work because God made His world to operate in a certain system. The "scientific method" is premised upon a stable universe, organized and ordered by The Creator. Universal laws are put in place to oversee activity of earthly relationships. The world functions premised upon the precision of God. Any observations or theories are attempts to characterize how God created His world. "Models" are human attempts to comprehend the "normal" and warn of the "catastrophic". Were the world in chaos, "normal" and "catastrophic" would change places.

4. Our proper response to the Creator is awe, humility, repentance, and worship.

Biblical Basis: Job 38-42; Psalm 8; Romans 1:18-32

You asked, "Who is this that obscures my counsel without knowledge?" Surely I spoke of things I did not understand, things too wonderful for me to know. Job 42:3

An anonymous man and woman pray over their bounty in a harvest field. The painter exactly captures the submissive response of people acknowledging The One Who provides all good things in life (Psalm 104). "Forgetting God" (e.g., turning away) creates inattention, apathy, *hubris*, and the thought of "look what I did" (Deuteronomy 8:10-20). Humans do well to consider their place in life: fallen, fragile, finite. Creation itself sets the rhythm of response—its every activity is seen as praise, adulation, and adoration (cf. Psalm 114:3-7; 148:1-13). If creation knows its place, it comes as no surprise that God puts us in ours. Human attempts to comprehend mystery, tension, and paradox produce "chaos" theories that suggest incompletion and inadequacy, creating dependence on God (Job 12:10).

HISTORY

1. History began in eternity.

Biblical Basis: Genesis 1:1; Ecclesiastes 3:10-11; Daniel 4:34-35; John 17:5, 24; Hebrews 1:1-2; Revelation 22:1-7

"And he made known to us the mystery of his will according to his good pleasure, which he purposed in Christ, to be put into effect when the times will have reached their fulfillment—to bring all things in heaven and on earth together under one head, even Christ." (Ephesians 1:9-10)

Biblically Integrative History: God is the author of history. God created all matter, space, and time but God does not wear a watch. He is not bound by time (cf. 2 Peter 3:8) since He is outside of and apart from time, but God has chosen to work within time to accomplish His plan. Jesus is the central person in God's plan and human history. Only He can, by His coming in the form of a man, bridge the gap between God's eternal kingdom and the temporal world (cf. Isaiah 9:6-7; Galatians 4:4-5). When studying history, we must frame our understanding of people, places, and events in the grand narrative of God's plan to make it meaningful. Apart from God, history is a meaningless record of man's vanity.

2. History has a purpose, an end in view designed by God.

Biblical Basis: Isaiah 14:26-27; 46:10-11; Daniel 2:20-23; Habakkuk 1-2; Ephesians 1:3-6,19-22; Colossians 1:15-18; Revelation 5:9-14

"For the earth will be filled with the knowledge of the glory of the Lord, as the waters cover the sea" (Habakkuk 2:14).

Biblically Integrative History: Human history has a beginning and an ending, a purpose, an ultimate destination. History does not "repeat itself." Though similar occurrences may be chronicled, God's ultimate plan for the world is Jesus' physical kingdom on Earth. God personally plans and oversees all the affairs of men. Nothing happens outside of God's design or purpose. All things are done for God's glory. God ordains the rise and fall of rulers and nations. The personal, eternal Creator is in control of the smallest detail to the greatest event. Though the flow of history may sometimes be a human mystery, all events are sovereignly interrelated.

3.   God's loving patience and righteous justice, form the bookends of history.

Biblical Basis: Judges; 2 Chronicles 36:15-23; Jonah; Habakkuk; Matthew 21:22-46; 2 Peter 3:8-10.

"The Lord, the God of their fathers, sent word to them through His messengers again and again, because He had pity on His people and on His dwelling place. But they mocked God's messengers, despised His words and scoffed at His prophets until the wrath of the Lord was aroused against His people and there was no remedy." 2 Chronicles 36:15-16

"The Lord is not slow in keeping his promise, as some understand slowness. He is patient with you, not wanting anyone to perish, but everyone to come to repentance." 2 Peter 3:8-10

Biblically Integrative History: God often brings about change that is slow but sure. Even though the consequences of one's action may not yet be fully evident, justice will come eventually (cf. 1 Timothy 5:24-25). The seeds of change may take time to germinate. God deals with nations and individuals according to their response to Him.   Israel's cycle of sin (Obedience, Disobedience, Judgment, Repentance, Deliverance) is a pattern that can be seen in the history of nations and individuals. God's character is that of a patient, loving father correcting and directing his son through life (cf. Proverbs 3:10, 11). Obedience to God's commands brings blessing, while continual disobedience and rejection of His commands brings God's righteous justice and judgment.

4. Memory is the basis for history. God expects us to learn about Him from past.

Biblical Basis: Deuteronomy 4:9, 10; 6:4-12; 8:10-20; Psalm 77:10-12; 78:1-8; 1 Corinthians 11:23-26

"I want you to recall the words spoken in the past by the holy prophets and the command given by our Lord and Savior through your apostles" (2 Peter 3:2).

Biblically Integrative History: Hebrews were taught to be "whole thinkers". To the Old Testament mind, the mental act of recall was supposed to be seamlessly linked with physical action. Remembrance led to recitation leading to public proclamation pointing to a memorial or holiday event. Acting upon statements of truth from the past was to consistently affect believers' conduct (Deuteronomy 13:1-3; 2 Timothy 1:13-14). Remembering how God has worked in the past should give one confidence about how He is working now. God's working in history reveals His character. Learning from past actions and mistakes can help people avoid repeating those mistakes.

LITERATURE

1. God initiated storytelling as a method of communicating truth.

Biblical Basis: Genesis 1:3 "and God said"; Deuteronomy 31:24; Romans 15:4; Revelation 13:8; 17:8

"All the days ordained for me were written in your book before one of them came to be" (Psalm 139:16).

Biblically Integrated Literature In eternity past, God "wrote books." His plan, worked out before creation (Ephesians 1:4), was

159

recorded before time (Revelation 13:8; 17:8). 40% of the Bible is narrative or story, showing how God communicated the most with His people. People write books since this is how God has expressed Himself. God's Book sets standards for reading books. The stories that people write should always be evaluated on the basis of God's story (cf. Deuteronomy 13:1-4; 1 John 4:1-6). Like everything else God created, stories can be corrupted. Truth and error can coexist within a tale that must be assessed by a believer with The Book (Hebrews 5:11-14). Stories can entertain, instruct, sooth, and anger based on the perspective of the author.

2. What is written with pen on paper is written on the human heart.

Biblical Basis: Genesis 6:5, 6; 8:21; Deuteronomy 6:5; 10:12-13; 11:18; Proverbs 4:23.

"For out of the overflow of the heart the mouth speaks" (Matthew 12:34).

Biblically Integrated Literature Every book is a statement of belief. People write what they believe. "The heart" (the Old Testament concept of the whole self, including the mind) is where belief originates. Love, sacrifice, hope, courage are collective human ideas expressed in literature. Depending on the author's intent, these themes may be an expression of godliness or sinfulness. The Christian, then, has the responsibility to recognize that if a writer writes truth it is a result of God's image stamped on their thinking (cf. Genesis 1:26-27; Romans 2:14, 15). If a writer writes falsehood it is a result of the corrupting influence of sin in the author's life (cf. Ephesians 4:17-19).

3. In stories, the battle of "good versus evil" is a result of human sin.

Biblical Basis: Genesis 3; Romans 3:9-20; Ephesians 2:1-3; Revelation 12:1-9

"He forgave us all our sins….And having disarmed the powers and authorities, he made a public spectacle of them, triumphing over them by the cross" (Colossians 2:13-15)

Biblically Integrated Literature One of the major themes in books is the war between "good" and "evil". People all over the world write about this struggle because the truth of it has affected everything and everyone from the beginning of time. When Christians read and think about these books there are some important principles to follow. (1) Evil is real, historical, and personal (Genesis 3:1-6; 1 John 3:8; Revelation 12:7-9). (2) There is no possibility that "evil" will ultimately win (Psalm 2; Colossians 2:13-15; Revelation 19:11-21). (3) "Evil" people follow the principles of "the evil one" (2 Corinthians 11:13-15; 1 John 3:10). (4) Any "good" thing comes from The Good God (Mark 10:17-18; James 1:17). (5) "Good" people follow laws, rules, and principles that come from The Good God (1 John 3:7, 9, 11-20). (6) "Good" always triumphs in the end because that is God's plan. While evil might gain the upper hand for a while from our limited human perspective (cf. John 12:31; 14:30; 16:11), wickedness will be vanquished by righteousness (Ephesians 1:20-22; Colossians 1:19-23; 1 John 3:8; Revelation 12:10-12).

4. Looking for a way out of trouble is the human search for freedom from the consequences of wrong choices.

Biblical Basis: Genesis 4; Job 9:32-35; Romans 5:12-19; 8:18; Revelation 21:1-7

"…I was overcome by trouble and sorrow. Then I called on the name of the Lord: O Lord, save me!" (Psalm 116:3)

Biblically Integrated Literature Sin has destroyed human harmony with God. So humans have need of salvation. Books are written which show the essential requirement that people have to have right relationships with each other and God. Books may not come right out and say that we have a need that can only be met by Jesus, but that is what they're looking for. Now people do not actively search for The One and Only True God (Romans 3:11) but

161

they look for a way to fill "the hole in their soul" (Ecclesiastes 3:11). People are hostile to God before they are saved (Colossians 1:21). But God offers faith and grace as gifts to reconcile people to Himself (2 Corinthians 5:18-21; Ephesians 2:8-10). Unlike redemption that is temporary in some books, only God's redemption (1) releases people from their wrongdoing (Titus 2:14), (2) is eternal (Hebrews 9:12), and (3) is dependant not on things or people but upon Jesus (1 Peter 1:18, 19).

Activity #9: "The Cultural Mandate" Principle
In Current Curricula

Directions: In addition to the subjects mentioned above, consider how the biblical principle of protection of and production from creation could be applied in you current scope and sequence.

Primary Grades

Animals: God told us to take care of the food we eat because we share what we eat with the animals (Genesis 1:28-30; Psalm 104:10-30).

Conservation: God told people to protect the mother animals so that they could raise their babies (Deuteronomy 22:6, 7).

Elementary Grades

Humane Shelters and Societies: Human beings are responsible to take care of animals, even if they don't belong to us (Exodus 23:5). God told us to rest one day a week and he expects people to treat the land the same way. God instructed people to keep land "fallow" every seventh year so that nutrients could be replenished (Leviticus 25:1-7). Similarly, crop rotation is imperative to maintain soil productivity, allowing some land to "rest".

Junior and Senior High Grades

Environmentalism: You cannot be, in good conscience, an evolutionist and environmentalist at the same time. The former believes "the strongest survive" while the latter understands "protection of the weak." These ideas are mutually exclusive. The Christian worldview provides the best basis for creation's care.

Business: Massive, overextended government intrusion into economic affairs (e.g. through taxation) hurts the private citizen more than it helps them (1 Samuel 8:10-18).

Other Potential Applications: Creational Issues; Physical Science; Business Practices; The Arts; Humanities; Agriculture; Industry.

163

Conclusion
Nothing But The Truth

In the movie *The Shawshank Redemption*, Tim Robbin's character has just returned from solitary confinement where he has been restrained for two weeks. At lunch his prison buddies ask him how he fared. "Easiest two weeks I ever did," came the smiling confirmation. As it turns out he 'took' music with him. When questioned whether or not the cell was equipped with a record player Robbin's replies, pointing to his head and chest, "No, it was in here." Expounding he says, "You need it so you don't forget that there's something inside that they can never take away...hope."

Only the Trinitarian Christian view of people and things gives eternal hope because we were made for another world. All beliefs, doctrines, philosophies, assumptions, and faith come down to this: *there is something else and Someone else outside of us.* In the Old Testament *hope* always referenced *certainty.* This desire was not how we use it when we say, "I hope the Cubs win the pennant this year!" Hebrew *hope* was defined as a certainty, an absolute, something that would happen without question, confidence based on expectation of future fulfillment. God had acted in the past; He would act in the future (Psalm 78:4-7). Because everyone believes something and trusts in someone (Psalm 39:7; Isaiah 8:17), there is a result. And Christian schoolteachers instruct toward that end (Psalm 130).

Hope forces us to say that everything is theological.[1] From the ceiling tile to the carpet fiber, from the green grass to the blue sky, from life to death, everything belongs to God. God is the source of all things (Psalm 93:1). Ideas, gifts, abilities, materials, humans, have The Creator to thank for their existence. God is the sustainer of all things (Psalm 104). Every breath we breathe, every

164

drop we drink, and every morsel we eat comes from The Almighty's beneficence. God will bring all things to a culmination (Isaiah 60-66, esp. 66:22). God's intention will be redeemed from Genesis one and two through Revelation twenty-one and twenty-two.

The opposite is also true: nothing is neutral.[2] There are no brute facts. God established the Creation order.[3] A stable universe is the basis for the scientific method as well as the fact that babies are born with the innate ability to suck. God established the common order.[4] What is true in one place at one time with one group is the same all over the world in any given generation. God established the commended order.[5] Since God made everything good, everything should be developed, enjoyed, and celebrated as God's good gift.

Scripture is clear that everything has been corrupted by sin (Romans 8:18-22). Sin is in us (Romans 6:11-14). Sin is not so much out there in the world, but in here, in our person. Sin is around us (2 Timothy 2:16-18). Sin influences personal choice and governmental policy (Proverbs 28:2-5, 12, 15-16, 28). Sin wars against the soul (1 Peter 2:11). Sin has marred, distorted, and warped creation (Genesis 3:14-19). Sin snatches life, debilitates life, replacing life with death (James 1:14-15). Our adversary who wants nothing more than our demise attacks what we eat, think, discuss, and teach (1 Peter 5:8-9).

At the same time, everything can be redeemed (Colossians 1:15-20). Creation can be reclaimed (2 Corinthians 5:16-21). Dance and song are captured for the celebration of our Lord and His world (Exodus 15:19-21; Psalm 149:3; 150:4). Creation can be reformed (Romans 12:1-2). Transformed thinking about mathematics honors the truthfulness, beauty, and pattern-oriented system of how our world works. Creation can be re-created (2 Corinthians 10:3-5). Committing spelling words to memory, establishing grammatical parameters for speech. Submitting debate to proofs of logic brings everything under the jurisdiction of Christ (Colossians 2:2-3). Creation will be renovated (Revelation 21:1-5). There will be *both* a new heavens *and* new earth. In anticipation of that day when everything from astronomy to zoology will be understood as God intended them to be, Christian schoolteachers act as "ambassadors of reconciliation" to reclaim God's working in His world for their students.

Scholastic reconciliation is entirely possible because, all truth is God's truth (Proverbs 8:12-36). Every fact or proposition has its source in God, no matter who says it or discovers it. Explanations of how babies or galaxies are born, is the domain of The Almighty who uses pediatricians and astrophysicists as His mouthpiece (cf. Job 38-41). John Calvin's comment is apt:

> Therefore, since it is manifest that men whom the Scriptures term natural, are so acute and clear sighted in the investigation of interior things, their example should teach us how many gifts the Lord has left in possession of human nature, notwithstanding of its having been despoiled of the true good.[6]

Four assumptions form the cornerstones of this distinctively Christian view of the world. (1) The Personal, Eternal Creator exists (Hebrews 11:1-3). (2) God has revealed Himself naturally and supernaturally (Psalm 19 and John 1:1-18). (3) Humans can know true Truth through God's world and His Word (Psalm 147:15-20). (4) God's Word interprets God's world (Titus 1:9-11). A Christian school must rest everything from its mission to daily lesson plans on these pillars for discovering God's truth.

If everything belongs to God then nothing is *secular*.[7] There is no such thing as *secular* music just as there is no such thing as *secular* physics. There is no *compartmentalization* of the spiritual, mental, physical, or social. We are whole people. The word *secular* must not be allowed to be pejorative or the antithesis of *sacred*. Otherwise we leave our students with the wrong impression; some things in God's world are *good*, others are *bad*. The Lordship of The Trinity blankets all of life. All things serve The Creator (Psalm 119:91). Whether appointing pagan kings for specific tasks (Isaiah 44:24, 45:1) or the day-night cycle (Jeremiah 33:25), everything is sacred—dedicated to Him.

Life's sacredness rests upon the premise that there is nothing outside God's constant control (Ephesians 1:9-11). Accomplishments in academics or athletics have their origin in

The Almighty who gives abilities and allows the results of any test or contest (Deuteronomy 6:10-12; 8:10-20; 1 Chronicles 29:14-16). Political maneuvering rests within the constraints that God sets up the "kingdoms of men and gives them to anyone he wishes" (Daniel 4:25). Incidents are not accidents. All things happen for a reason whether we understand them or not (Job 42:1-6). Relationships, human or cosmic, are ordered by the unseen and sometimes misunderstood plans of God (Job 37:6-13; 38:22-30).

If all of life is sacred, there is nothing outside God's personal interest (Ecclesiastes 5:18-20). Work, intended by The Creator from the beginning, became corrupt, yet still essential for life, will be reinstated for all eternity (Genesis 2:15; 3:17-19; Isaiah 65:21-23; Acts 3:21; Revelation 22:3). The product of one's labor is protected because property is sacrosanct (Exodus 22:1-15). Language bridges differences. So important is this to God that His Gospel was disseminated to variant languages all at once (Acts 2:1-11) and all people groups will be included in God's kingdom (Revelation 5:9-10).

There is nothing outside God's active involvement (Isaiah 46:9-11). Science is simply the observations of God's management of His world (Job 26). There is nothing over which Jesus does not declare, "I am Lord" (1 Timothy 6:13-17). Administration, business, physical education, speech, technology, drama, spelling, vocabulary, literature, and social studies—all of education belongs to God. He organized His world to be known by and lived in by the crown of His creation: human beings. T.S. Eliot summarizes the importance of our collective concerns:

> ...if we define the purpose of education, we are committed to the question "What is Man for?" Every definition of the purpose of education, therefore, implies some concealed, or rather implicit, philosophy or theology. In choosing one definition rather than another, we are attracted to the one because it fits in better with our answer to the question "What is man for?"[8]

"Why did Jesus heal people if He knew they were going to die anyway?" Great question! And the answer follows the pattern of wholeness. Jesus' healing ministry while on earth was a marker, a precursor of the restoration His salvation brought. As obvious proof of His deity, Jesus showed through His miracles the priority of what was important: the completion of body and matter with soul and spirit. Jesus healed as a pointer that humans are whole people, not pieces and parts. Other views of life are confused, conflicted, and contradictory—true fairy tales. Cosmic redemption is found solely in the resurrection of Jesus from the dead, destroying the power of sin, sickness, and death. Only the Christian worldview holds out a coherent, comprehensive, compelling hope for this life and the next. Herein is the basis for biblical integration in the Christian school.

Appendix One
On The Same Page: Definitions of Integration

Everyone must begin on the same page. The definition of biblical integration cannot be one thing to one person and another to someone else. There have been many Christian educators who have spoken on this topic. When we weigh their words carefully the essence or core is the same though their descriptions may differ.

Arthur F. Holmes maintained that Christian education was not "good education plus good atmosphere", but engendered positive Christian contributions to the arts and sciences. Approaches that could be taken to produce classroom integration include (1) the teacher's Christian attitude toward learning, (2) ethical issues, (3) foundational beliefs, and (4) worldview studies.[1] Later Holmes suggested that we refer to this process of Christian thinking as "reintegration" because the original, intentional union of God in creation was broken at the fall.[2]

Frank E. Gaebelein agreed saying that the word "integration" simply meant bringing the parts into the whole directed by an external, eternal source of truth that drew all truth together in unity.[3] United together in a single unit is how Ronald P. Chadwick stated the case.[4] Harro Van Brummelen concurred by arguing that "the harmony of faith-based learning results in an integral whole."[5] This unifying perspective must come from the source of truth, God, in His Word, maintains George R. Knight.[6] So Scripture must contain the insights that govern interpretation of Christian school curriculum.

Producing educators who will do the job is the concern of Kenneth O. Gangel. He asserted that Christian teachers must know the scriptures intimately, study the culture diligently, and analyze events and issues theologically, adopting a set of distinctively Christian presuppositions.[7] Likewise, James D. Cunningham and Anthony C. Fortosis argued that integration was to be transformational, relational, professional, practical, and maturational for the Christian instructor.[8] Apart from Christian change and interaction with disciplines, biblical integration would not take place.

Practicing the philosophy of biblical integration has begun in some circles understanding exactly the ideas mentioned above.[9] Preserving a stringent definition of biblical integration will ensure that Christian education will interact with the world Christ came to redeem, under the supervision of divine revelation.

Appendix Two
Hermeneutics of Integration

A school said that women could not wear men's clothing. The basis for that startling declaration is supposedly confirmed by Deuteronomy 22:5. But what did that statement *mean* for the original hearers? Is the Christian design for women's attire limited to western style skirts and dresses? The dress code of this particular Christian school had no other Old Testament reference cited save this one.

In a Christian school history class 1 Chronicles 7:14 is promoted as a statement of need for America claiming the United States as 'God's people' whose land God will 'heal' based on nation wide repentance. Was not this a statement directed at Israel? While none would argue the prominence of America as a nation in human history, only non-Jewish states such as Assyria, Egypt, and Edom had whole Old Testament books or passages directed at correcting their national policies.

Jeremiah 29:11 hangs as a banner citing the Bible verse selected by the graduating class of a certain Christian school claiming that God "has a plan to prosper" those individuals. Why has no one chosen Jeremiah 18:11 that claims God's plan to "destroy" His people? Do Christians have the hermeneutical right to pick and choose biblical citations that fit their liking while dismissing others by remaining mute concerning their existence?

Examples of misinterpreted and misapplied Scriptures could be multiplied. The point in such a serious undertaking of practicing biblical integration is clear: interpretation of Scripture necessitates rules. Yet, problems of interpretation persist. No one should appropriate God's Word making it mean what he may want it to mean. Application to current time must follow interpretation of what a passage meant in the past. Principles to live life must not be seen as coming off the top of someone's head. While this volume does not purport to be a hermeneutical textbook, this appendix is necessary to provide a framework from which to use principles found herein and to allow other principles to be understood from the text of Scripture.

The Problems of Context

Humans are finite, limited by time and space. Problems of interpretation, then, are bound by calendar and geography, including:

1. *Knowledge*: 21st century people do not necessarily know more or even better than some who lived in the second millennium B.C.
2. *History*: Moderns have much to learn from those who lived before us. We cannot think that we "have arrived" while the laws of the past are considered relative and time-conditioned.
3. *Culture*: Though technologically advanced, our society should not be necessarily held as the standard over our predecessors. How people dress, eat, or sing does not make one group better than another.[1]
4. *Testament*: To jettison the Old Testament as antiquated or out-of-date provides dangerous precedent for the removal of the New in our own day. If the Old Testament provided groundwork for the early Church in its own ethical system, it cannot be dismissed as irrelevant for any reason. All of God's Word is profitable[2]. Therefore, the 21st century Christian should take great care in deriving principles from either testament.[3]
5. *Context*. To lift any passage out of its immediate surrounding verses is to eliminate the sense of the original writer. An interpreter of the Scriptures should be careful to view the passage within its context and substitute its original meaning with a different one.

Biblical Principles as Universal for All Peoples

Creation ordinances, such as procreation, management of resources, or work and rest, are practiced worldwide, as established for humanity in Genesis 1 and 2. Wisdom literature also shows the complementary nature between nations, based upon a transcendent standard.[4] Ubiquitous medical, political, and judicial codes in the 21st century mirror the Old Testament canon's pronouncement, "man is made in the image of God" endowing him with inalienable rights.[5] These elemental precepts provide a broad base for the widespread scope of Scriptural law codes relating to all people in all places for all time.[6]

Canaanite cultures were destroyed because of breaking God's laws (Leviticus 20:23, 24). Proverbs 11:14 states that nations fall for a lack of guidance while Proverbs 14:34 declares, "righteousness exalts a nation." The godless nation of Assyria repented of their sin against The Personal Eternal Creator after hearing the evangelical message of Jonah (3:1-10). The Old Testament, though written to the Hebrews, was germane to and, at times, composed directly for Gentile nations:

- Genesis 3   The sin of two people affected the
                       whole human condition.
- Genesis 6-9   The sin of whole earth brought
                       judgment on the whole earth.
- Genesis 11   The sin of unified humanity judged
                       all people.
- Genesis 12:1-3   The whole earth would be blessed
                       through Hebrews.
- Genesis 13:1   Five pagan cities "sinned greatly
                       against The LORD."
- Genesis 18:20   The sin of ungodly Sodom and
                       Gomorrah was "grievous."
- Genesis 18:25   God is referred to as "the judge of all
                       the earth."
- Isaiah 13-23   Various nations are judged by God.
- Jeremiah 45-51   Various nations are judged by God.
- Ezekiel 25-32   Various nations are judged by God.
- Daniel 2 and 7   Various nations are judged by God.
- Amos 1-2   Various nations are judged by God.
- Obadiah   Edom is judged by God.
- Jonah   Assyria is judged by God.
- Nahum   Assyria is judged by God.

In each of these cases, the standard for the nations is the righteousness of God. God considered all people from every nation as important, calling them to repentance and rejoicing (e.g., Psalms 96-100). God testifies to people of Himself through the witness of creation (Psalm 19), conscience (Romans 2:14-15), human law (Deuteronomy 4:5-8; 1 Timothy 1:8-11), miracles (2 Kings 5) and the attraction of believers (Ruth 1:16, 17; 1 Kings 10:1-9). Even God's judgments were designed specifically to demonstrate to other nations that "there was no one like Yahweh in all the earth" (Exodus 9:13-21; cf. Daniel 4:28-37). And His people were to bear the light of "the gospel" to others (e. g., Genesis 12:1-3; Exodus 19:5, 6; Deuteronomy 4:5-8; 1 Kings 10:1-9, 24; Ecclesiastes; Isaiah 42:6; 49:6). There is hope for all nations, even in the afterlife (Isaiah 19; Zechariah 14:16-19; Malachi 1:5). If the ethical codes of the Old Testament are not universal in scope, then we limit the transcendence of the "Creator of the ends of the earth" (Isaiah 40:28).

Biblical Principles as Continual for All Time

"That's in the *Old Testament!*" is sometimes issued as a statement of non-application. The contention would be that the first covenant, the first testament is outdated. It is correct that specific statements arguing for or against some of the positions taken by Christians in a given social setting do not always exist in the Old Testament. Principles governing athletics, artistic endeavor, reading extra-biblical books, or having a gold standard for a nation's economy cannot always be detailed by individualized chapter and verse. However, without Genesis through Malachi, indeed, Genesis 1-11, present day believers would have no foundation for their worldview. For example, without the literal, historical events of Genesis 3 there is no necessity for appeasing The Father's wrath through The Son's sacrifice for human redemption. Some claim the creation account in Genesis to be myth—a human story to understand our origins. However, if The Fall of Man did not take place in history, there is no need for The Person of Christ to physically, literally eradicate the penalty for human transgression on the cross. As Diagram #20 illustrates, without those first eleven chapters of the Bible the rest of Scripture would be unnecessary.

Diagram #20

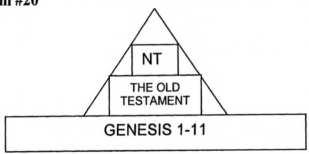

New Testament ethics are based on Old Testament ethics. Racism finds its first prohibition in Genesis one when The Godhead declares that all people are image bearers of Him. A pro-life stance against abortion builds on God's image finding basis for human proliferation in Genesis chapters one, five, ten, and eleven as a command from on high. Concerns for so-called *environmental problems* originate in the cultural mandate that gives humans responsibility for preserving creation (Genesis 1:28). Evolution, and its violent implications through social-Darwinianism, is a direct attack upon the creation and its Creator. The first argument for capital punishment finds its foundation in Genesis nine. Governmental structure is premised upon humans following strictures established beginning in the second chapter of Genesis. Crime is wrong. Genesis 3 is the basis for police departments, trial lawyers, and judicial systems. The 10 commandments[7], a pillar for New Testament ethics, is preceded with the words, "I am The LORD your God who brought you out of Egypt"; though Christians are not specifically addressed, we twenty-first century onlookers take these ethics as our own. Even the first command of Exodus 20 finds its law dependent upon the first chapter of Genesis. The base for all teaching in both testaments is founded in Genesis 1-11.

Two controls mediate the complexity of transferring principles from one period of time to another: progressive revelation and the ideal and the real. As God gave more revelation over time a greater responsibility was brought to bear on the hearers of successive generations (cf. John 16:12, 13; Hebrews 1:1, 2). Jesus' denunciation of Jewish unbelief compares the Hebrews of His day to the vilest of Old Testament populations saying that Sodom and Gomorrah would have repented had they had the revelation available to Capernaum, Bethsaida, and Corazin (Matthew 11:20-24). Peter discovered that Old Testament dietary law had been altered by God (Acts 10). Paul would explain many passages from the Old Testament making direct application to his audience (cf. 1 Corinthians 9 where laws governing dietary intake for animals are shown to have specific appliance to humans). More revelation brought more responsibility.

Given all this direct revelation from God, one would think following His precepts would bring heaven to earth. But there is that small issue of human sin. The effects of God's Word on His world are not easily transferred from one time to another or from Word to action because of human corruption. Even though it's impossible to create the ideal, it is the model we are to attempt. Note the following definitions:[8]

- THE IDEAL: God's standard. God never compromises His own perfection or the righteousness required for salvation (thus Jesus' death on the cross for human sin). God's immutability is intact. *While not lowering His Standard, God lowers Himself, stooping to our level so as to save us from ourselves.*

- THE REAL: God's condescension. God's standard is not compromised, *but it is conditioned because of corrupted human thought and action.* These laws, then, allow for the imperfection of people. God's intention is to *limit and lessen the consequences of human behavior.* This is yet another example of divine grace and mercy.

For example, Malachi records that God hates divorce (2:16) and yet Deuteronomy 24:1-4 proscribes rules that allow the practice. In the ancient world women were often treated as chattel or property. The Old Testament, then, became a beacon of light giving Hebrew women protection against domineering men. Jesus himself said that the only reason for allowance of divorce laws was because of the stubbornness of God's people (Matthew 19:8, 9).

Of course Exodus 20 commands that no one "kill" another. The idea of that Hebrew word connotes "premeditated murder". However, Numbers 35:6-34 limits the punishment of a person who *without intention of malice* kills another by establishing "cities of refuge". The Old Testament distinguished between murder and manslaughter premised upon the *intent* of the person. In a sinful, imperfect world it would be hard to know a person's mind. So the Old Testament law *erred* on the side of mercy giving the dictate to modern courts that one is innocent until proven guilty. While there was great hardship upon the one who killed unintentionally (e.g. separation from family and livelihood) in the event of the high priest's death the manslaughter *count* would be dropped, setting a time limit on the penalty (Numbers 35:27-28; see also Deuteronomy 19).[9]

Application of the ideal and real may incorporate the age-old adage that, "There's more to it than meets the eye". As a case in point, to help cities cut down on the spread of AIDS some health departments pass out clean syringes to people in known drug havens. Is this a good or bad practice? Abiding by the premise that teenagers will do it anyway, schools pass out condoms in class to prevent unwanted pregnancies. Is this a positive or negative policy? Some communities are tired of public profanity and pass laws to punish those who swear in civic locations. Is this right or wrong? A poem might communicate an apt note of conclusion:

Sin Distorts.
Man Cavorts.
Law Resorts
To rules and courts,
To give society
Realistic Supports,
Keeping people from
Getting out of Sorts.[10]

Biblical Principles are Applicable for All Situations

"So what? Who cares? What does it mean for me today?" are the three questions students of every generation raise. Jesus used the phrase "as it is written" again and again to show the Old

177

Testament's authority in His day. In His temptation (Matthew 4:1-11) the application was directly personal. For questions of social concern, such as divorce, Old Testament law was clear (see the above discussion). And for those who would find ethical *loopholes* in the law, Jesus made the loophole into a noose (cf. Mark 7:9-13)! Paul said to Ephesian church elders that he preached, "what would be helpful", and declared to them, "the whole counsel of God," from the Old Testament (Acts 20:20, 27). Elsewhere, the apostle directs that the Old Testament was for, "endurance and encouragement" (Romans 15:4), setting an example (1 Corinthians 10:1-11), and that it was for our profit (2 Timothy 3:14-17). Since our Lord and the apostles found the Old Testament principles to be binding on everyday life, the codification of law in both testaments still has relevance in our century. The law provides regulations for civil peace and security (1 Timothy 1:8-11), commands for personal responsibility (Ephesians 6:2-3), and ethics from one culture to another (1 Timothy 5:18).

What are the steps necessary for understanding a book that was written at another time for another people yet still applies today?

1. *Context: What did it mean for them, then?* History, culture[11], linguistics, genre[12], and immediate context must be examined.
2. *Correlation: What does the rest of Scripture say?* Beginning with the passage being studied, to the author of the book, and ultimately to the other 65 books; comparison and contrast further elucidates the breadth of meaning.
3. *Principalization: What general rule is understood?* While the specifics of time and place change, the truth of the law never does.
4. *Application: How does the universal rule relate to the present?* Relevance and function might include a multiplicity of specific and exact ways in which this principle is practiced in present day.
5. *Personalization: How will I specifically and individually practice this principle?* People want to know how truth works in real life, right now.[13]

The principle of Sabbath rest from Leviticus 23:3 could be used as an example. Israel was receiving the law prior to their taking possession of the land. God says that there is to be a day of sacred assembly or literally a convention day, a day of celebration. But celebration of what? The command harkens back to the creation. God fixed the precedent setting a standard for all creation. Not only were people (including slaves!) to rest, but also the animals (cf. Exodus 20:8-11). The day was one of celebration because it had significance. God said to remember that life had meaning because He made it. The phrase, "wherever you live," suggests that there were no geographical or cultural boundaries. A collective worship of The Creator was to take place wherever Israel called home. And it was "a Sabbath to The Lord" implying that the focus was on God not the people. Contemplation of who He is and what He has done will lessen the siren's call of other gods.

Important for remembrance and also for rest, God set specific governors for Sabbath living. The command, "There are six days you may work," limits the mandate to rule the earth. The fruit of one's labor was not the end all for life. The rule, "you are not to do any work," was a release, not a restriction. God is not a killjoy but The Personal Creator gives that we might enjoy. Law is given with peoples' best interests at heart (cf. Deuteronomy 30:11-16). "The seventh day is a Sabbath rest" literally means a 'rest, rest.' Hebrew doubling of words was a literary device for emphasis. Taking a break increased focus on God and exponentially bettered the physical production for the next week. God knew what He was doing.

Holidays[14] also had a purpose. They created memories (leaving Egypt, Leviticus 23:42-43), reminded people of their place (God is the 'landlord', 25:23), established repetition (for generations to come, 23:41), formed memorials (benefiting descendents, 23:33, 42), and produced anticipation (the possibility of release from debt, 25:10). The rest of Scripture heralds further ideas not already mentioned: The Sabbath was a sign between God and His people (Exodus 31:12-17); blessing resulted from keeping the day (Deuteronomy 15:1-11), treating Sabbath like any other day was grounds for chastisement (Nehemiah 13:15-22), the Sabbath was made for people (Mark 2:20-28), and external

179

appearances were no way to judge a person's activities on the Sabbath (John 7:21-24; cf. Colossians 2:16-23).

The Sabbath was meant as a humanitarian principle, an economic, philanthropic benevolence with the focus being concern for others. Abuse and misuse, as with any God-given gift, can prove to be harmful, however. We must guard our Sabbaths for they are assistance from God and we must guard against turning gifts into whips. So, as a general principle, a creation ordinance for all people, perhaps another poem would suffice to define the principle:

> God gave a special day,
> Because people are made of clay,
> So that believers could pray,
> And all people could play.

Application to present day life is obvious. Perhaps a series of questions for reflection would prompt the student of Scripture. For whom do I work? Why do I work? Do I restore, refresh my fatigue? Is my leisure time spent pouring myself into something else? Are my "Sabbaths" tuned to reflection, refocus, repose, and relaxation? Do I remember why I come to church services on Sunday morning? Do I remember why Sunday is special? Do I remember why I am a Christian? Am I busying myself so much on Sunday with church activities that my rest turns to rush? Do I put on a front, an appearance of being O.K., but inside I am empty and miserable? What do I do with my free time? Do I waste time or use time? Am I giving my family and friends a grumpy view of life? Do they see me enjoying or enduring life? Do I know the Lord of the Sabbath any better today than I did yesterday?

Specific practice of Sabbath will differ for everyone. Cutting firewood and clearing brush might be 'just the ticket' for someone with a sedentary vocation such as being an educator. Sitting behind a desk all week might prompt some to rest by working in the yard or planting a garden on their Sabbath. Others might spend time with family inside and outside of their homes. Still others might reconsider their treatment of people or their love of things over people because of this law. Mini-retreats, personal days, or goal-setting might lend them to further the process more than one day a week just as Israel had many opportunities to reconnect past action with present reality.   The following responsive reading might lend itself to further contemplation on the principle of sabbath.

May I Make Time to Rest, Lord

Lord, when the alarm clock, stove clock,
and time clock demand my presence,
When the pace of life is hectic,
When I wish there were six more hours in a day,
When the traffic light is stuck on red,
And my family's schedule demands I be
in three places at one time,
May I make time to rest, Lord.

Lord, when people expect too much of me,
When the boss has forgotten about the eight-hour day,
When I am constantly at others' beck and call,
When the cell phone, pager, fax, and email
all go off at once,
And I begin to hate the human race,
May I make time to rest, Lord.

Lord, when work occupies all my waking hours,
When television commercials say I must have more,
When my neighbors flaunt their newest toys,
When alcoholic does not apply but workaholic does,
And I decide to go to the office on Sunday to catch up,
May I make time to rest, Lord.

Lord, when money means more than people,
When I read *The Wall Street Journal* more than my Bible,
When overtime becomes my primetime,
When promotions and pay hikes are my ultimate goals,
And "looking out for number one"
has become my slogan in life,
May I make time to rest, Lord.

Lord, may I refocus my life on you.
May I restore my thoughts in your Word,
May I refresh my schedule
by meditating on all your blessings,
May I relax my activity every week
to enjoy the life you gave me,
May I make time to rest, Lord.

Resources

Books, series, websites, periodicals, and articles are offered as suggestions to Christian educators for help in further developing a biblical view of subject areas below. This is *not* a bibliography, nor is this inventory exhaustive.

Biblical Integration

Banks, Robert and Stevens, Paul R. *The Complete Book of Everyday Christianity.* Downers Grove, IL: InterVarsity Press, 1997.

Beck, W. David, ed. *Opening the American Mind: The Integration of Biblical Truth in the Curriculum of the University.* Grand Rapids: Baker, 1991

Biblical Integration Posters: math, science, history, literature, language arts, and fine arts posters for home and classroom use. www.biblicalintegration.com

Biblical Integration Resources www.biblicalintegration.com offers a free monthly e-zine addressing important issues related to Christian education and Biblical integration as well as numerous Biblical integration resources for teachers including audiotapes, books, and posters.

Blamires, Harry. *The Christian Mind.* Ann Arbor, MI: Servant, 1963.

Chadwick, Ronald P. *Christian School Curriculum: An Integrated Approach.* Winona Lake, IN: BMH Books, 1990.

Chadwick, Ronald P. *Teaching and Learning: An Integrated Approach to Christian Education.* Old Tappan: Revell, 1982.

Colson, Chuck and Pearcey, Nancy. *How Now Shall We Live?* Carol Stream, IL: Tyndale, 1999.

Council for Christian Colleges and Universities. www.cccu.org

Critique: Helping Christians Develop Skill in Discernment. www.ransomfellowship.org

Dockery, David S. & Thornbury, Gregory Alan. *Shaping a Christian Worldview: The Foundations of*

Christian Higher Education. Nashville: Broadman & Holman, 2002.

Eckel, Mark. *Biblical Integration: The World Through The Word*. Self-published, 1996.

Gaebelein, Frank E. *The Pattern of God's Truth: The Integration of Faith and Learning*, reprint, Colorado Springs: ACSI, 1999.

Gangel, Kenneth O., ed. *Toward a Harmony of Faith and Learning: Essays on Bible College Curriculum*. Farmington Hills, MI: William Tyndale College Press, 1983.

Garber, Steven. The Fabric of Faithfulness. Downers Grove, IL: InterVarsity Press, 1996.

Gill, David W. *The Opening of the Christian Mind*. Downers Grove, IL: InterVarsity Press, 1989.

Greidanus, Sidney. "The Use of the Bible in Christian Scholarship". *Christian Scholars Review* XI:2 (March, 1982), pp. 138-147.

Guides to the Major Disciplines Series. Intercollegiate Studies Institute, 1997.

Hasker, William. "Faith-Learning Integration: An Overview". *Christian Scholars Review* XXI:3 (March, 1992): 231-248.

Holmes, Arthur F. "Integrating Faith and Learning in a Christian Liberal Arts Institution, " in *The Future of Christian Higher Education* , David S. Dockery, ed. (Nashville: Broadman & Holman, 1999), pp. 155-172.

Holmes, Arthur F. *Building The Christian Academy*. Grand Rapids: Eerdmans, 2001.

North, Gary. *Foundations of Christian Scholarship: Essays in the Van Til Perspective*. Ross House Books, 1976.

Olasky, Marvin. *The Turning Point Series*. Wheaton, IL: Crossway Books, 1987.

Plantinga, Cornelius. *Engaging God's World: A Christian Vision of Faith, Learning, and Living*. Grand Rapids: Eerdmans, 2002.

Smith, Robert W., ed. *Christ and the Christian Mind*. Downers Grove, IL: InterVarsity Press, 1972.

Through the Eyes of Faith Series. San Francisco: Harper & Row, 1985.

Van Dyk, John. *The Craft of Christian Teaching: A Classroom Journey*. Sioux Center, IA: Dordt Press, 2000.

Walsh, Brian J. and Middleton, J. Richard. "Bibliography". *The Transforming Vision: Shaping a Christian Worldview*. Downers Grove, IL: InterVarsity Press, 1984.

Wolters, Albert M. *Creation Regained: Biblical Basics for a Reformational* Worldview. Grand Rapids: Eerdmans, 1985.

WORLD Magazine www.worldmag.com

Hermeneutics and Biblical Integration

Dyk, Elmer, ed. *The Act of Bible Reading: A Multi-disciplinary Approach to Biblical Interpretation*. Downers Grove: InterVarsity Press, 1996.

Fee, Gordon D. & Stuart, Douglas. *How to Read the Bible for All It's Worth: A Guide to Understanding the Bible*. Grand Rapids: Zondervan, 1982.

Goldingay, John. *Approaches to Old Testament Interpretation*, rev. ed. Downers Grove: InterVarsity Press, 1990.

Hendricks, Howard G.; Hendricks, William D. *Living By The Book*. Chicago: Moody Press, 1991.

Kuhatschek, Jack. *Taking the Guesswork out of Applying the Bible*. Downers Grove, InterVarsity Press, 1990.

Longman, Tremper III. *Making Sense of the Old Testament: Three Crucial Questions*. Grand Rapids: Baker, 1998.

McQuilkin, J. Robertson. *Understanding and Applying the Bible: An Introduction to Hermeneutics*. Chicago: Moody Press, 1983.

Sandy, D. Brent & Giese, Ronald L. Jr. *Cracking Old Testament Codes: A Guide to Interpreting the Literary Genres of the Old Testament*. Nashville: Broadman and Holman, 1995.

Virkler, Henry A. *Hermeneutics: Principles and Processes of Biblical Interpretation*. Grand Rapids: Baker, 1981.

Webb, William J. *Slaves, Women & Homosexuals: Exploring the Hermeneutics of Cultural Analysis*. Downers Grove: InterVarsity Press, 2001.

Best, Harold M. *Music Through the Eyes of Faith.* Harper & Row, 1993.

Books and Culture Magazine. www.christianitytoday.com.

Eckel, Mark. *The Pagans Are Coming: Using Non-Christian Materials in The Christian School.* Self-Published, 2001.

Gaebelein, Frank E. *The Christian, The Arts, and Truth.* Sisters, OR: Multnomah, 1985.

Guinness, Os. *The Devil's Gauntlet.* Downers Grove, IL: InterVarsity Press, 1989.

Kavanaugh, Patrick. *The Spiritual Lives of Great Composers*, rev. ed. Grand Rapids: Zondervan, 1996.

Mangalwadi, Vishal & Ruth. *The Legacy of William Carey.* Wheaton, IL: Crossway, 1999.

Mars Hill Tapes, with Ken Myers. www.marshillaudio.org.

Mattingly, Terry. "What Kind of Missionaries Are We?" *Moody Monthly*, September, 1992, pp. 38, 88.

Myers, Ken. *All God's Children And Blue Suede Shoes.* Wheaton, IL: Crossway, 1989.

Niebuhr, Richard. *Christ and Culture.* San Fransisco: Harper, 1951.

Olasky, Marvin. "Studying Babylon" *WORLD* 24 February 96, p. 30.

Ryken, Leland. *Culture in Christian Perspective.* Sisters, OR: Multnomah, 1986.

Romanowski, William D. *Eyes Wide Open: Looking for God in Popular Culture.* Grand Rapids: Brazos, 2001.

Romanowski, William D. *Pop Culture Wars: Religion and the Role of Entertainment in American Life.* Downers Grove, IL: InterVarsity Press, 1996.

Smith, Jane Stuart and Carlson, Betty. *A Gift of Music: Great Composers and Their Influence.* Wheaton, IL: Crossway, 1978.

Spenser, William and Aida. *God Through the Looking Glass: Glimpses of the Arts.* Grand Rapids: Baker, 1998.

Turner, Steve. *Imagine: A Vision for Christians in the Arts.*
Downers Grove, IL: InterVarsity Press, 2000.

West, John G. Jr. "Nineteenth-Century America." in
*Building a Healthy Culture: Strategies for an American
Renaissance.* Donald Eberly, ed. Grand Rapids: Eerdmans, 2001,
pp. 181-199.

Wolfe, Christopher. "The Moral Grounds for Advancing
Cultural Health: Whose Standards? in *Building a Healthy Culture:
Strategies for an American Renaissance.* Donald Eberly, ed.
Grand Rapids: Eerdmans, 2001, pp. 115-136.

Literature and Language in Biblical Integration

Cowan, Louise & Guinness, Os. *Invitation to the Classics.*
Grand Rapids: Baker, 1999.

Gallagher, Susan V. and Lundin, Roger. *Literature
Through the Eyes of Faith.* Harper & Row, 1989.

Guroian, Vigen. *Tending the Heart of Virtue: How Classic
Stories Awaken a Child's Moral Imagination.* Oxford, 1998.

L'Engle, Madeleine. *Trailing Clouds of Glory.*
Philadelphia: Westminster, 1985.

Larsen, David L. *The Company of the Creative: A
Christian Reader's Guide to Great Literature and its Themes.*
Grand Rapids: Kregel, 1999.

Lockerbie, D. Bruce. *Dismissing God: Modern Writers'
Struggle Against Religion.* Grand Rapids: Baker, 1998.

Pearce, Joseph. *Literary Converts: Spiritual Inspiration in
an Age of Unbelief.* Ft. Collins, CO: Ignatius, 1999.

Priestley, J. B. *Literature and Western Man.* San
Fransisco: Harper, 1960.

Progeny Press. Christian Literary Guides to The Classics.
www.mgprogeny.com

Ryken, Leland. *The Christian Imagination.* Grand Rapids:
Baker, 1981.

Ryken, Leland. *Realms of Gold.* Harold Shaw, 1991.

Ryken, Leland. *Windows to the World.* Grand Rapids:
Zondervan, 1985.

Smith, David I. and Carvill, Barbara. *The Gift of the Stranger: Faith, Hospitality, and Foreign Language Learning.* Grand Rapids: Eerdmans, 2000.

Veith, Gene Edward. *Reading Between the Lines.* Wheaton, IL: Crossway, 1990.

Math and Science in Biblical Integration

Alberda, Willis, "Existence in Mathematics," *Pro Rege,* March, 1979, pp. 11-15.

Alberda, Willis, "What is Number?" *Pro Rege,* March, 1975, pp. 2-8.

Answers in Genesis. www.answersingenesis.org

Berndt, Chard. *Biblical Classification of Life: A Framework and Reference for Authentic Biblical Biology.* Filer, ID: ElihuPublishing, 2000.

Butler, Diana, "God's Visible Glory: The Beauty of Nature in the Thought of John Calvin and Jonathan Edwards," *Westminster Theological Journal* 52 (1990), 13-26.

A Christian Perspective on The Foundations of Mathematics. Proceedings of the Conference held at Wheaton College, April 28-30, 1977.

Cosgrove, Mark P. *The Amazing Body Human.* Grand Rapids: Baker, 1981.

Durrant, Laurice, "Teaching a Research Course from a Christian Perspective—Integrating Faith with Learning," in *Christ in the Classroom: Adventist Approaches to the Integration of Faith and Learning,* vol. 1, Silver Spring, MD: The Institute for Christian Teaching, 1991, pp. 47-64.

Graves, Dan. *Scientists of Faith.* Grand Rapids: Kregel, 1996.

Howell, Russell W.& Bradley, W. James. *Mathematics in a Postmodern Age: A Christian Perspective.* Grand Rapids: Eerdmans, 2001.

Institute for Creation Research. www.icr.org.

McMillen, S. I. *None of These Diseases.* Revel, 1967.

Nickel, James. *Mathematics: Is God Silent?* Vallecito, CA: Ross House Books, 1990.

Pearcey, Nancy R. and Thaxton, Charles B. *The Soul of Science: Christian Faith and Natural Philosophy*. Wheaton: Crossway, 1994.

Ross, Hugh. *The Creator and the Cosmos*. NavPress, 1993.

Tiner, John Hudson. *Champions of Science*. Green Forest, AR: Master Books, 2000.

Tiner, John Hudson. *Champions of Math*. Green Forest, AR: Master Books, 2000.

Reasons to Believe. www.reasons.org.

Zimmerman, Larry L. *Truth & The Transcendent: The Origin, Nature, & Purpose of Mathematics*. Florence, KY: Answers in Genesis, 2000.

History in Biblical Integration

Boorstin, Daniel. *The Discoverers*. New York: Random House, 1983.

Butterfield, Herbert. *Christianity and History*. New York: Revel, 1949.

Buttrick, George A. *Christ and History*. Nashville: Abingdon, 1963.

Cahill, Thomas. *How the Irish Saved Civilization*. New York: Doubleday, 1996.

Johnson, Paul. *Intellectuals*. San Fransisco: Harper, 1988.

Marsdan, George and Roberts, Frank, eds. *A Christian View of History*. Eerdmans, 1975.

Schaeffer, Francis *How Should We Then Live?* Good News Publishers, 1983.

Swanson, Roy. *History in the Making*. Downers Grove, IL: InterVarsity Press, 1978.

Weaver, Richard M. *Ideas Have Consequences*. Chicago: University of Chicago, 1948.

Notes

Preface

1. Terry Anne White, *The Life of George Washington Carver*. (New York: Landmark, 1957), p. 102.
2. See Appendix #1 "On the Same Page" pages 169-170.
3. Appendix #2 "The Hermeneutics of Biblical Integration" is meant as a self-regulator, an overseer of the process followed herein.

Introduction

1. Art Marquardt, "New Americans," *Toledo Blade* 25 December 1994, G: 1.
2. Michael Logan, "The Greatest Story, Retold," *TV Guide*, 6 May 2000, p. 18.
3. Vaclav Havel, "Forgetting We Are Not God," *First Things*, 51 (March, 1995), pp. 47-50.

Chapter One

1. "Don't Blame the Supreme Court," *Chicago Tribune*, 15 December 2000, p. 28.
2. Joel Belz, "Everything is Faith-Based," *WORLD*, 21 April 2001, p. 5.
3. Eric Burns, "Bias, Witting and Unwitting, Among the God's of Journalism," *Fox News Watch Online*, 31 May 2001.
4. Similarly, if the group decides what is right or wrong, problems remain. If majorities rule, minorities lose their voice (or their heads, as in the French Revolution). Other countries should not criticize tyrants terrorizing a nation if each is only responsible to himself.
5. Possible counter statements might include: people regardless of age do wrong; if we do wrong we should admit it; people create television and books and people are sometimes wrong; making excuses for doing wrong shows how wrong we are.

6. Alston Chase, "Harvard and the Making of the Unabomber," *Atlantic Monthly*, June, 2000, p. 50.

Chapter Two

1. Some key passages on doctrine being important for the Christian are Matthew 7:28, 29; Acts 2:42; Romans 16:17; 1 Timothy 6:20-21; 2 Timothy 4:2-5; Titus 1:9; Hebrews 13:9, 10.
2. Some, of course, refuse to acknowledge God's truth (Isaiah 45:4; Jeremiah 9:3, 6; Romans 1:18-32; 2 Timothy 3:7).
3. Mark Eckel. *Timeless Truth: An Apologetic for the Reliability, Authenticity, and Authority of The Bible.* Teacher's Resource Guide. (Colorado Springs: ACSI, 2001), pp. 6-7.

Chapter Three

1. It is important to acknowledge that people pick and choose pieces of different beliefs adding them to their own worldview "grocery cart." This is called syncretism. People literally *whirl* their views, creating a spiritual amalgam. "At this early stage, we're seeing a mix-and-match religion....People believe, but not in the dogma of an institutionalized religion. They take a piece of Buddhism, a piece from the cabalas, a piece of the Bible and they form it for their own lifestyle and beliefs." Gerald Celente, Director, Trends Research Institute, Rhinebeck, New York, quoted in "Spiritual Marketplace: Traditional Religious Institutions Adjust to Meet Consumer Demand," by Connie Lauerman, *Chicago Tribune* 24 May 2000, pp. 1, 4. Actress Sarah Michelle Gellar is a good example. "I consider myself a spiritual person," she told Scotland's *Daily Record*. "I believe in an idea of God, although it's my own personal ideal. I find most religions interesting, and I've been to every kind of denomination: Catholic, Christian, Jewish, Buddhist. I've taken bits from everything and customized it." *Christianity Today*, 8, July 2002, p. 10.
2. Thomas Cahill, *The Gifts of The Jews*, (New York: Doubleday, 1998), pp. 156-57.
3. Rachael Kessler, "Nourishing Students in Secular Schools," *Educational Leadership,* December, 1998/January, 1999, p. 49.

4. "Good" pluralism suggests that everyone be listened to; "bad" pluralism demands everyone be believed (often leaving out the exclusive Christian viewpoint).

5. Pauline B. Johnson, "Art", *Christ and the Modern Mind,* Robert W. Smith, ed. (Downers Grove: IVP, 1972), p. 72.

6. Suggestions might include: (1) God, Providence, Sovereignty (2) Creation, Sin (3) Heaven/Hell, Eternal Life (4) Decree of God, Instruction, Memory (5) Creator, Sustainer, King (6) God's Law (7) Truth, Discernment (8) Corrupt nature (9) Rationalization, Passing the Buck, Blame, Shame (10) God's image, Holy Spirit (11) Image of God (12) Judgment.

Chapter Four

1. Some refer to the human sin problem as "total depravity." Isaiah 64:6 is clear: "our righteousness acts are like filthy rags." We can never achieve right relations with God on our own. The phrase may be misunderstood, however, if people think that we are as bad as we can be or that we are incapable of any "good" act. At the same time, while even motivations are corrupt, people do "good things" (cf. Acts 10:2, 4, 22).

2. This is why authors of Scripture refer to "hidden faults" (cf. Psalm 19:12), asking The Almighty to "search" them to see if there is any wickedness in them (cf. Psalm 139:23, 24). Only God can correctly judge each individual because only The One who made us can see us for what we are (cf. 1 Corinthians 4:3-5; Hebrews 4:12, 13).

3. Moore, Frazier, *"Lolita*: Decide for Yourself," *Mattoon (Ill.) Journal Gazette*, 6 August 98, C5.

4. Chuck Colson's 1993 Templeton Award Address.

5. See Elijah Wald and Ruth Hubbard. *Exploding the Gene Myth: How Genetic Information Is Produced & Manipulated by Scientists, Physicians, Employers, Insurance Companies, Educators, & Law Enforcers.* Beacon Press, 1994. D.D. Jackson, Joel Schwartz, and S. Robert Lichter. *It Ain't Necessarily So: How the Media Remake Our Picture of Reality.* Penguin, 2002.

6. Evan Thomas, "The Day That Changed American," *Newsweek* 21 December 2001/7 January 2002, pp. 40, 42.

7. Ron Rosenbaum, "Staring into the Heart of Darkness: Evil Is Back," *New York Times Magazine*, 4 June 1995, 41, as quoted by Ravi Zacharias, *Deliver Us From Evil* (Dallas: Word, 1996), 174.

8. Elise Wachspress, "Evil Can Happen in Your Neighborhood," *Chicago Tribune,* 27 December 2001, p. 17.

9. Some people struggle with serious problems that are not simply remedied by a few trite statements. Two extremes should be avoided: (1) no one should use declarations such as these as excuses for wrong behavior; (2) no one should think that learning disabilities are overcome with simplistic statements of truth or simple adjustments to behavior. While we act toward students as whole people who may respond through different treatments, we must understand that biology or environment have been equally deformed by The Fall. Jesus' words "what comes out of a man makes him unclean" (Mark 7:20-23) should be one of the doctrinal markers for addressing learning difficulties as an issue first and foremost of corrupt human nature.

10. Luke wanted his readers to check his story (Luke 1:1-4; Acts 1:1-3). "Check it out for yourself" should be the watchword in the Christian school (Acts 17:11)!

Chapter 5

1. We were alienated from God and were enemies in our *mind* (Colossians 1:21), but now God puts His laws in our *mind* (Hebrews 8:10), so that we will love Him will all our *mind* (Mark 12:30), that we might be transformed by the renewing of our *mind* (Romans 12:2).

2. Charles Habib Malik, *The Christian Critique of the University.* Downers Grove, IL: InterVarsity Press, 1982, p. 112.

3. Ken Gangel, "Biblical Integration: The Process of Thinking Like a Christian," *The Christian Educator's Handbook on Teaching*, (Scripture Press, 1988), p. 76.

4. Chuck Colson, "An Interview with Chuck Colson, " *Covenant Online*, 2:2, pp. 1-2. Though Mr. Colson's attention was directed toward Christian colleges, the same concerns could be voiced of all Christian schools.

5. Pages 152-162 give basis for the core courses of mathematics, science, history and literature based on work done for *Biblical Integration Posters*, www.biblicalintegration.com.

6. Frank Gaebelein, "Toward a Philosophy of Christian Education," *An Introduction to Evangelical Christian Education*, ed. By J. Edward Hakes, (Chicago: Moody Press, 1964), pp. 40-41.

7. Steve Stanek, "Religious Schools Draw Wider Flock," *The Chicago Tribune*, 15 April 2001, 17:11.

8. Suggestions might include, (1) "Whoever is forgiven much has the best lawyer", (2) "The greatest will be the greatest", (3) "Fear physical death, the end of our existence", (4) "Peace at all costs", (5) "Claw your way to the top", (6) "Toot your own horn, no one else will", (7) "I want as much as I can get as fast as I can get it".

9. Suggested responses to some might be (11) Is the latest educational philosophy or establishment dictating "new" directives for teachers? Some times the Christian community bows before the totem of pagan thinking because we want to "stay current," "be recognized," or be an alternative rather than a distinctive kind of school. (15) Are we still learning and growing? Have we become stagnant in the pursuit of truth and knowledge? Moving away from legalistic practices, allowing non-Christian dramatic productions, could be an example. (16) Are we blind to the falsehood of tradition over truth? Do we do what we do because we've always done it this way or do we acknowledge that we might not know it all? (20) Like the rest of creation, primary colors are limited by the confines God established. Boundaries and precincts of operation in color allow for a multiplicity of hues, shades, and tints within a God-set structure.

Chapter Six

1. "Integration" is often misunderstood as putting Bible verses *into* teaching. Contrarily, the word suggests bringing everything together as one. "Synthesis" is the best English word to communicate the concept, but the phrases "biblical integration" or "faith and learning" are so ingrained within Christian school education that to change the expression would likely cause confusion.

2. 'Principalization' is "that procedure which seeks to discover the enduring ethical, spiritual, doctrinal, and moral truths or principles which the writer himself set forth by the way in which he selected his details and arranged the contextual setting of his narrative. Principalization seeks to bridge the "then" of the text's narrative with the "now" needs of our day; yet it refuses to settle for cheap and quick solutions which confuse our own personal point of view (good or bad) with that of the inspired writer." Walter Kaiser, *Toward an Exegetical Theology*, (Grand Rapids: Baker, 1981), pp. 150-63, 197-98. The methods of identifying biblical principles will be noted, as will multiple examples.

3. Mark and Tyler Eckel. *Things That Go Bump in the Night: Frankenstein, Horror and The Christian School.* Unpublished. 2002.

4. See Appendix One, "Definitions of Biblical Integration." While scholars and practitioners may *describe* biblical integration one way or another, the essential *definition* remains the same.

5. "Illustration" takes a thought or incident or a character in a story, for instance, to show an example or demonstration of truth. For example, "This subject is *like* when the Bible says..." or "Just *as* the Bible talks about pruning vineyards, so we should take care of our plants..." These examples give the implication that comparison or metaphor is biblical integration. It is *not*.

6. See Appendix Two, "The Hermeneutics of Biblical Integration." The Bible is not something we *use* to get an answer. Scripture speaks and we are responsible to listen. Interpretation of God's Word cannot be done casually.

7. Biblical integration *is* recognizing that God's construction of human kind establishes blood as the life source which is clearly stated in Leviticus 17:11 and 14.

8. Seoul Foreign School, for instance, serves a great number of business and ambassadorial families in the capital city of South Korea. Pressing needs, here as elsewhere, center on hiring teachers who can suffuse their teaching with biblical assumptions, moving their students down-the-line of salvation.

9. It should be noted that while many believe in *en loco parentis*—in place of the parent—as their operational basis, others would see home, church, and school as separate "spheres".

Jurisdiction and authority would remain with each entity rather than school's existence being dependant upon support of the home.

10. James Orr. *The Christian View of God and the World as Centering in the Incarnation.* (New York: Scribners, 1897), pp. 10-11.

11. *The Hymnal 1982.* (New York: The Church Hymnal Corporation, 1985), hymn # 412.

12. Ceremonial, ritual, or metaphorical associations of water in Scripture, however, do not fulfill the requirement to identify water's essence, role, or operation such as in John 7:38 or Ephesians 5:26.

13. Jesus argued based on words (John 10:34), a word (Matthew 22:43), and the tense of a verb (Matthew 22:32). Our Lord stated that the smallest letter or distinguishing mark producing different letters would be kept safe (Matthew 5:17-19; Luke 16:17). 2 Thessalonians 2:13-15 indicates that words communicated in person or in letter bore "truth". 2 Timothy 3:16 states that all scripture is God breathed and 2 Timothy 1:14 commands us to guard the good deposit entrusted to us.

14. In biblical thought, correction or discipline was goal oriented. Godly development of the individual was the target (cf. Proverbs 1:2-3; 8:10; 2 Timothy 3:16; 4:2).

15. The Old Testament concept of "distinction" through holiness (cf. Leviticus 10:10-11) is mirrored in the New Testament concept of "progressive growth" through sanctification (cf. Philippians 3:12-15).

16. As God's agents in creation, believers are responsible to uphold God and His Law (Genesis 1:28), submit to structures of government (Genesis 9:5-6), justly administrate the affairs of life (Deuteronomy 17 and 19), recognizing people placed by God in positions of authority to whom we are liable (cf. 1 Thessalonians 5:11, 12; 1 Timothy 2:2; Hebrews 13:17).

17. Dan Graves. *Scientists of Faith.* (Grand Rapids: Kregel, 1996), pp. 117-120. Along with *Doctors who Followed Christ* (Grand Rapids: Kregel, 1999), Graves has provided a documented resource in math and science demonstrating how many great discoveries were borne out of a Christian worldview.

18. G. Ronald Murphy. *The Owl, The Raven, and The Dove.* (Oxford: University Press, 2000).

19. Eric Metaxas. *Squanto and the Miracle of Thanksgiving.* (Nashville: Tommy Nelson, 1999).

20. I am indebted to my colleague Sue Howard for bringing Hardy's beliefs to my attention.

21. D. Bruce Lockerbie. *Dismissing God: Modern Writers' Struggle Against Religion.* Grand Rapids: Baker, 1998.

22. Writing a course motto in six to ten words could be the "catch phrase" for the class. For instance, math mottos might include, "Postulates are truth from heaven to earth" or "Designer numbers, eternal functions." Literature mottos might include, "Reading books by The Book" or "There is truth in fiction".

Chapter Eight

1. I am indebted to my colleague Cheri Smith for this observation.

2. See chapter 1.

3. A Christian view of what lies ahead includes this world and the next (cf. Philippians 2:21-26; 3:12-14, 20-21; 4:10-20).

4. Discussed in detail in chapter 1.

5. I am indebted to my colleague Rae Jean Belt for pointing this book out to me.

6. In more recent editions, the original chapter seven has been extracted from the story.

7. Mary Cowan and Os Guiness, eds. *Invitation to the Classics.* (Grand Rapids: Baker, 1999).

8. C. John Sommerville. *How the News Makes Us Dumb: The Death of Wisdom in an Information Society.* (Downers Grove: IVP, 1999).

9. See pages 31-35.

10. The Hebrew word indicates that people can make God's name vain, empty, without merit. The statement written to Israelites warns them as God's people that trivializing the character of God by taking Him lightly is a serious offense. The same could be said of Christians who lose the fear of God, flippantly acknowledging The Almighty without humility, sanctity, or trembling.

11. The famous legend of Pygmalion and Galatea set the premise for Shaw's work. *My Fair Lady* is the popularized version of the story today.

12. The Greek word for "test" is important. Romans had a counterpart to the modern mall called the *agora*—a marketplace containing various vendors. A potter would bring his wares to sell. An astute consumer would lift the pottery holding it against the light of the sun to see if any cracks had been filled with wax that week while the potter fired his pots. In the same way, John says Christians are to hold variant worldviews to the light of the Scriptures, exposing the cracks, insufficiencies, and outright deceptions of purveyors of "truth" in the marketplace of ideas.

13. Eckel, *Timeless Truth*, Teacher's Resource Guide, pp. 267-269.

14. Robert W. Smith, ed. *Christ and the Modern Mind*, (Downers Grove, IVP, 1972) p. 49.

15. Possible subject areas could include history and a discussion of the "Just War Theory", business law and insurance, economics and poverty, health and cleanliness, construction and safety codes, etc. Christian communication in the classroom might include, "Christian groups that show people how to farm, dig wells, or build hospitals in other countries helps them to sustain lives in their country and the life of their country."

16. Possible subject areas could include Bible and Jesus' anger over our enemy death in John 11:33, the responsibility humans have for their physical body in life, the renovation of earth and our new body, accounting principles and wills, the application of math in the production of bombs, etc. Christian communication in the classroom might include, "Preparing their spirit for eternity with Christ and preparing their inheritance for their children are both responsibilities Christians take seriously."

17. Possible subject areas could include the lack of editing in writing with the advent of email and spell checking, cars grant freedom of travel while taking us away from home, spending time with people over many years versus the tendency to move when "we don't like something", etc. "Christian communication in the classroom might include, "Staying in one Bible teaching church while living in a community shows family commitment."

Chapter 9

1. Mark Eckel. *Biblical Integration: Understanding the World Through The Word.* (Self-published, 1996-2001), p. 4-6.

2. See Ronald L. Koteskey, "An Integration of Statistics and Christianity", *Journal of Psychology and Theology* 3 (1975) Summer, 195-201; Laurice Durrant, "Teaching a Research Course from a Christian Perspective—Integrating Faith with Learning," *Christ in the Classroom: Adventist Approaches to the Integration of Faith and Learning, vol. 1, pp. 47-64.* David Murray, Joel Schwartz, and S. Robert Lichter, *It Ain't Necessarily So: How Media Make and Unmake the Scientific Picture of Reality.* Penquin, 2002.

3. Excellent articles posing serious questions about polling include: Jerry Adler, "The Numbers Game", *Newsweek* 25 July 1994, pp. 56-58; Fred Barnes, "Can You Trust Those Polls?", *Reader's Digest,* July, 1995, pp. 49-54; Les Sillars, "Governed by Gallup?", *WORLD,* 27 March 1999, p. 21, whose questions were the basis for comments under number two.

4. Adapted from an assignment by Katie Hefft in Methods 1, Moody Bible Institute, 8 October 2001.

5. Adapted from an assignment by Lisa Willms in Methods 1, Moody Bible Institute, 8 October 2001.

6. Adapted from an assignment by April Anderson in Methods of Math and Science, Moody Bible Institute, 2 December 1999.

7. Adapted from an assignment by Cara Clark in Methods of Math, Moody Bible Institute, 13 November 2000.

8. Ideas suggested from an assignment by Terri Houston in Methods of Math and Science, Moody Bible Institute, 13 November 2000.

9. Adapted from an assignment by Erika M. Sweeting in Methods 1, Moody Bible Institute, 20 October 1999.

10. Originally developed for a self-published book *Biblical Integration: Understanding the World Through The Word* (Mark Eckel, 1997), these core course philosophies for biblical integration (including additional related concepts, attitudinal objectives, and classroom application activities) are now available

in poster form at <u>www.biblicalintegration.com</u> (© 2002 Mark Eckel and Douglas Osborn).

11. *Course of Study for Christian Schools* (Grand Rapids: Eerdmans, 1947), prepared for the National Union of Christian Schools, is an out-of-print work that exactly accomplishes this task.

Conclusion

1. The phrase "all things" occurs throughout Scripture. God gives life to all things (Nehemiah 9:6; 1 Timothy 6:13) and all things are created for, by, and through Him (cf. Proverbs 16:4; 26:10; John 1:3; Colossians 1:16, twice). Indeed Paul desired Jesus to have preeminence in all things (Colossians 1:18). Everything is theological because everything belongs to and is sustained by The Triune God.

2. Psalm 24:1; 50:12; 89:11. There is no such thing as "non-alignment" or "non-partisan" in God's world.

3. Ephesians 1:21 says Jesus is "far above all rule and authority" meaning that passages such as Romans 13:1, Ephesians 3:10, Colossian 1:16, and 1 Peter 2:13-14 show Christ alone gives the power for all authorities or systems to exist or function—whether government officials or the law of gravity.

4. Psalm 64:9; 65:8; 66:4; 67:1-7. All people in all places and times have recognized that there is One and Only True God who causes men to "ponder what He has done" (64:9).

5. Genesis 1:10, 12, 21, 25, 31; 1 Timothy 4:4-6. God made everything good.

6. John Calvin, *Institutes of the Christian Religion*, reprint. (Grand Rapids: Eerdmans, 1997), 2.2.15.

7. Psalm 148:1-12. "The general legislation of Leviticus shows that all life is lived under the watchful eye of God, and as a result it makes no artificial differentiation between what is holy and what is secular. A holy people will by their lives transform mundane things into beautiful and acceptable offerings to God...The underlying aim of the teaching is thus to ensure that God's holiness will be able to regulate and direct every area of human activity...the character of these ordinances shows that all aspects

of life under God are sacred." R.K. Harrison, *Leviticus: An Introduction and Commentary* (Downers Grove, IL: Inter-Varsity Press, 1980), pp. 32, 120.

8. T.S. Eliot, "The Aims of Education," *To Criticize a Critic* (New York: Farrar, Straus & Giroux, 1965), pp. 75-76.

Appendix 1

1. Arthur F. Holmes, "Integrating Faith and Learning," *The Idea of a Christian College*, rev. ed. (Eerdmans: 1987), pp. 45-60.

2. Arthur F. Holmes, "Integrating Faith and Learning in a Christian Liberal Arts Institution," in *The Future of Christian Higher Education*, David S. Dockery, ed. (Nashville: Broadman & Holman, 1999), pp. 155-172.

3. Frank E. Gaebelein. *The Pattern of God's Truth: The Integration of Faith and Learning.* (Chicago: Moody Press, 1974), pp. 7-13.

4. Ronald P. Chadwick. *Christian School Curriculum: An Integrated Approach.* (Winona Lake, IN: BMH Books, 1990), p. 30.

5. Harro Van Brummelen. *Steppingstones to Curriculum: A Biblical Path.* (Seattle: Alta Vista College Press, 1994), p. 129.

6. George R. Knight. *Philosophy & Education: An Introduction in Christian Perspective*, 2nd. Ed. (Berrien Springs, MI: Andrews University Press, 1989), p. 208.

7. Kenneth O. Gangel, "Biblical Integration: The Process of Thinking Like a Christian," *The Christian Educator's Handbook on Teaching: A Comprehensive Resource on the Distinctiveness of True Christian Teaching.* (Victor Books, 1988), pp. 74-86.

8. James D. Cunningham and Anthony C. Fortosis. *Education in Christian Schools: A Perspective and 'Training Model'.* (Whittier, CA.: ACSI, 1987), pp. 173-174.

9. For example, *Toward a Harmony of Faith and Learning: Essays on Bible College Curriculum*, Kenneth O. Gangel, ed. Farmington Hills, MI: William Tyndale College Press, 1983 and *Shaping a Christian Worldview: The Foundations of Christian Higher Education*, David S. Dockery & Gregory Alan Thornbury, eds. Nashville: Broadman & Holman, 2002.

Appendix 2

1. The theocratic economy of the Old Testament is no longer in force. While God is still Lord over all creation The Church is God's people, not a specific country. Some systems of government follow biblical guidelines, for instance. A republic reflects God's rule of law over against a totalitarian dictatorship. However, a monarchy may well manage law just as righteously as a democratically elected congress.
   2. Cf. Romans 15:4; 1 Corinthians 10:1-11; 2 Timothy 3:16.
   3. Imagine a text for friendship based on Amos 3:3!
   4. Compare Proverbs with Egyptian hymns, for instance. At times the only difference is the name of God. If all truth is God's truth we should not be surprised to find it everywhere.
   5. Examples could include The Hippocratic Oath, The Geneva Convention, and international treaties.
   6. The following disclaimers must also be stated: (1) the established ethic may or may not produce the intended result (Proverbs 15:1; 26:4, 5), (2) there may be exceptions to the rule (Proverbs 22:6) and (3) the ethic is dependent upon human implementation (Proverbs 16:10).
   7. Jesus did not come to abolish The Law but to fulfill it (Matt 5:17) because the law is "holy, just and good" (Rom 7:12). Specific items have been eliminated because of ceremonial usage (e.g., Eph 2:15), legalism is reviled (e.g., Rom 9:31) and salvation by works of the law is never ordained in Scripture (e.g., Rom 3:21, 28). But then, we ask and answer with Paul, "Do we, then nullify the law by this faith? Not at all! Rather, we uphold the law" (Rom 3:31) because we are a slave to God's law (7:25) based upon the sacrifice of Jesus! Christians are called to fulfill the Old Testament law of brotherly love (Jas 2:8). Sin is referred to in John's epistle as "transgressing the law" (1 John 2:7, 8, 23, 24; 5:2, 3).
   8. I have written on this elsewhere, first in *Biblical Integration: Understanding the World through The Word* (Self-published, 1996-2001) and *Timeless Truth: An Apologetic for the Reliability, Authenticity, and Authority of The Bible, Teacher's Resource Guide* (Colorado Springs: ACSI, 2001), pp. 131, 263, 324.